BACON FREAK

50 Savory Recipes
for the Ultimate Enthusiast

Rocco Loosbrock, Sara Lewis & Dawn Hubbard

STERLING EPICURE
New York

STERLING EPICURE
New York

An Imprint of Sterling Publishing Co., Inc.
1166 Avenue of the Americas
New York, NY 10036

ISBN 978-1-4549-1851-6

Distributed in Canada by Sterling Publishing Co., Inc.
C/o Canadian Manda Group, 664 Annette Street
Toronto, Ontario, Canada M6S 2C8
Distributed in the United Kingdom by GMC Distribution Services
Castle Place, 166 High Street, Lewes, East Sussex, England BN7 1XU
Distributed in Australia by NewSouth Books
45 Beach Street, Coogee, NSW 2034, Australia

For information about custom editions, special sales, and premium and corporate purchases, please contact Sterling Special Sales at 800-805-5489 or specialsales@sterlingpublishing.com.

Manufactured in China

2 4 6 8 10 9 7 5 3 1

www.sterlingpublishing.com

To my best friend and wife of 22 years. Yaneth, thank you so much for supporting my delicious love affair with bacon.

—Rocco "Boss Hog" Loosbrock

Contents

CHAPTER 1

Why Bacon?

It's been said that "Bacon makes everything better." It's the truth! Bacon does make everything better. Bacon makes all foods better, and because food is life, bacon makes life better, too.

This simple bacon belief has caused bacon mania to sweep the nation. Why has bacon become so popular? The simple answer is this: because it smells and tastes so darn good. That smoky aroma, that crispy texture, and that oh-so-heavenly taste! When you have something as addictive and umami-laden as bacon, a cultlike following is only natural. But its taste is not the only thing that has made bacon so trendy.

Bacon has infiltrated the strata of pop culture on every level. Second only to cats in its ability to go viral across the Internet, bacon has become a beacon of hope to a nation of hungry carnivores, meatatarians, and even vegetarians who occasionally need to indulge their animal instincts. Coincidentally, you can't spell *beacon* without b-a-c-o-n.

Bacon has slipped free of its "unhealthy" reputation and has been embraced by proponents of the Atkins and Paleo™ diets and P90X® and CrossFit fanatics. Bacon is now championed by everyone from the super fit to the super fat and everyone in between. As more studies emerge showing that fat is not the worst food it was once thought to be, more and more people are wholeheartedly embracing a high-fat diet. In fact, bacon has so many health benefits, we've dedicated a whole section of this book to them.

Bacon is a "luxury" food that everyone can afford to indulge in. For many people, it's a comfort food, a guilty pleasure, "the way to a man's heart" and an aphrodisiac (or so we've heard). Perhaps that is why bacon is so symbolic of "'Merica." Our collective love of bacon unites us as a nation. In the melting pot and sizzling skillet that is America, if there's one thing that brings us all together, it's bacon.

BACON BITS

In a survey conducted by Maple Leaf Foods, 23 percent of men said that the aroma of bacon was their favorite fragrance.

Bacon Freak is a cookbook for today's bacon fan. Consider this list of people who find bacon irresistible: foodies, chefs, hipsters, bloggers, nerds, jocks, home cooks, health nuts, exercise freaks, sports fans, beauty queens, hikers, bikers, truckers, sheep herders, cowboys, cowgirls, moms, dads, kids, dogs, and anything with the ability to smell.

Who We Are

Baconfreak.com and Bacontoday.com were founded on the simple principle that a world of bacony goodness exists out there for all to discover and enjoy. Here's what we know to be true:

* The most versatile meat on the planet deserves some respect.

BACON BITS

BACON has been trendy since 1708! In Ebenezer Cooke's 1708 poem *"The Sot-Weed Factor,"* a satire of life in early colonial America, the narrator observes that most of the food in America is bacon-infused.

**Rocco and Yaneth Loosbrock say,
"Bacon has cleaved us together."**

* Bacon is a treat for all the senses.
* Breakfast is not the only meal for bacon.
* There's no limit when cooking with bacon.
* As some folks have said, bacon is meat candy!

In our heart of bacon-wrapped hearts, we're just a bunch of Bacon Freaks. Just like you. We're firm believers that bacon is not just the most awesome food on the planet, but that it's the most entertaining food, too! With bated bacon

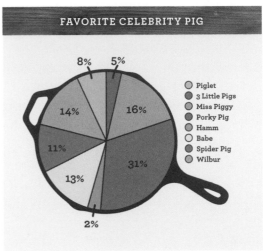

FAVORITE CELEBRITY PIG

- Piglet
- 3 Little Pigs
- Miss Piggy
- Porky Pig
- Hamm
- Babe
- Spider Pig
- Wilbur

8% 5% 16% 14% 11% 13% 2% 31%

breath, we've watched bacon's triumphant rise in popularity and its unsurpassed ability to go viral across all social media outlets. If there was ever a food worthy of superhero status, it's bacon (now *that's* a summer blockbuster we'd like to see). Bacon even has its own holiday!

We believe there are no limits when it comes to creatively cooking with bacon. If you think you've seen it all when it comes to experimenting with bacon in the kitchen, we're here to tell you that you ain't seen nothing yet! They say the sky's the limit, but with bacon's soaring success, we've proved that pigs really can fly. We've made it our lifelong mission to explore strange new bacon pairings, to seek out new flavors and new combinations, to boldly go where no bacon has gone before.

Our recipes are easy to follow for cooks of all skill levels, and we don't use any high-falutin' ingredients. We're sure that some chef somewhere is doing amazing things with bacon and sea urchin, but that's just not our style. You've probably never seen recipes like these, but you'll definitely want to get your greasy hands on them.

Recipes are ranked on a scale of difficulty from one to five bacon strips. One bacon strip means it's incredibly simple; five strips mean it's approaching "epic" status. But don't worry, we respect bacon way too much to waste it in a recipe that'll make a YouTube video go viral, but that you wouldn't want to eat. The only bacon recipe worth making is one that's worth eating.

Since it's been proven that bacon does make everything better, this bounteous book of bacon will include recipes for breakfast, lunch, dinner, dessert, and everything in between. Our recipes call for traditional American bacon that comes from the belly of the hog. There's no lamb bacon, no Canadian bacon, no fakin' bacon, and absolutely no turkey bacon used in these recipes here, so put down the prosciutto and back away slowly . . .

And boy oh bacon are we delivering the dessert recipes! If there's one thing we (and our Bacon Today fans) love, it's the sweet, salty, savory combination of bacon + chocolate. If you think it sounds weird (we're pretty sure you're not one of *those* people, but just in case), all we can say is, don't knock it until you've tried it! In fact, stop reading right now and go make one of them. Go on now. Why are you still here?!

We'll also be putting our bacon expertise to good use. For each recipe, we'll suggest a Bacon Freak bacon that we feel best brings out its flavor. We've even got a suggested boozy beverage pairing for every recipe that doesn't already have booze or beer in it. And the bacon doesn't stop there. Consider these pages your one-stop shop for all things bacon. Now enjoy, and get your freak on!

We've been in the bacon business since 2001. It's true; we actually drove the proverbial bacon bandwagon long before it went electric. We liked bacon before it was cool. We're the bacon masterminds behind the #1 online bacon store Baconfreak.com and the #1 bacon blog Bacontoday.com. For over a decade, we've influenced bacon's rise

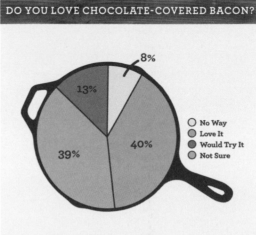

DO YOU LOVE CHOCOLATE-COVERED BACON?

8%

13%

40%

39%

○ No Way
◐ Love It
● Would Try It
◑ Not Sure

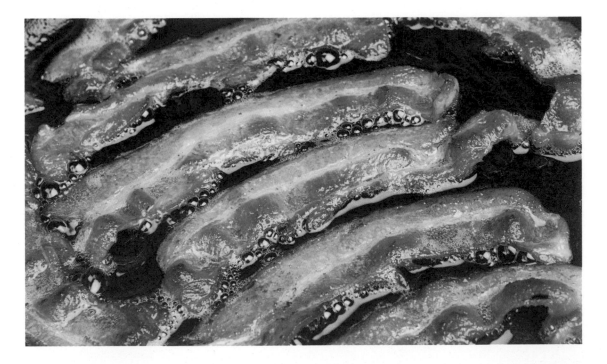

BACON BITS

A two-hundred-pound* pig will yield approximately twenty pounds of bacon.

in popularity. We coined the "Bacon is Meat Candy" motto. We were the first company to create Bacon Jerky (you're welcome). We've been with bacon on every step of its journey. It's our job to come up with fun, innovative, and delicious bacon recipes and we're tickled piggy pink to be an authority on bacon. It's the best job in the world!

Our "Bacon Is Meat Candy" Bacon of the Month Club was one of the first bacon delivery services, and is now the oldest. We deliver packages of delicious bacon to the homes of bacon fans all across the United States and Canada. When it comes to cooking with bacon, the quality of the bacon is what makes all the difference. Bacon Freak bacon is dry-cured using a traditional method. Since launching our first bacon club 13 years ago, we've developed more than 3 dozen different types and flavors of bacon to help our customers explore as many different bacon varieties as possible. Getting creative with bacon is just another job perk.

CHAPTER 2

Bacon 101

Makin' Bacon

Do-it-yourself is all the rage. Canning is making a comeback. Home brewing and winemaking are totally trendy. Even making your own cheese and yogurt and raising hens for fresh eggs are gaining in popularity. One of the benefits of this DIY trend is that old-fashioned butcher shops are popping up around the country, which makes it a lot easier to purchase uncured pork bellies for making your own bacon at home. You can also find pork bellies from local farms and grocery stores. For the true bacon aficionado, who worships bacon and wants to be involved in every aspect of the makin' bacon process, you can't beat home-cured bacon.

DRY-CURING VERSUS WET-CURING

There are two ways to cure bacon, either by dry-curing or by wet-curing. The wet-cure method involves immersing the meat in a liquid brine that consists of salt, sodium nitrate, sugar, and water. It is then refrigerated for several days. This method is common in mass-market food production. Industrial pork producers inject the bacon with the brine solution instead of submerging it in the brine. This is why it's possible to find bacon where the first (and most abundant) ingredient on the label isn't bacon; it's water! No joke. Oh, the horror!

This injection of brine results in bacon

*Throughout this book we use imperial measurements (cups, teaspoons, tablespoons, quarts, inches, pounds, and °F). For those of you who prefer metric measurements, we've included a handy Metric Conversions chart on page 166.

that shrinks and shrivels when you cook it. If you aren't sure whether you have this type of bacon in your fridge, you'll know as soon as you cook it. There will be lots of splatter and, even worse, the meat will shrivel up into tiny strips that once resembled bacon. Many people think it's the fat in bacon that causes splatter, but it's actually the added water that causes it. We all learned in fifth-grade science class that oil and water don't mix. Add heat to that and soon you've got a fireworks show in a frying pan. For these reasons, we

do not recommend wet-curing bacon, and most people curing bacon at home prefer the dry-cure method. How do you spell delicious? Dry-cured bacon.

The dry-cure method is a time-honored tradition that dates back thousands of years. The earliest references to bacon curing date back to China, circa 1500 BCE. Dry-curing bacon has been a vital method of meat preservation since before the invention of refrigerators or electricity. Dry-curing gets its name from the fact that all the ingredients used in the curing process are dry. Brine and water are never injected into the meat.

All varieties of Bacon Freak bacon are dry-cured. There are many advantages to this method. The first is that there is hardly any shrinkage to the slices when cooking dry-cured bacon. When you cook a pound of dry-cured bacon, you'll get (almost) a pound of bacon. Try seeing how much bacon you end up with after cooking a pound of wet-cured bacon from the grocery store! You'll be shocked to discover how much of that weight is just water. Another advantage to dry-curing is the flavor. Dry-cured bacon simply tastes much better than wet-cured bacon and is the ideal bacon to use as an ingredient in a recipe. And because there is no water or brine, there's a lot less splatter when you cook it. That's why we say dry-cured bacon is the only bacon you can fry naked! Go ahead and try it. We don't judge here.

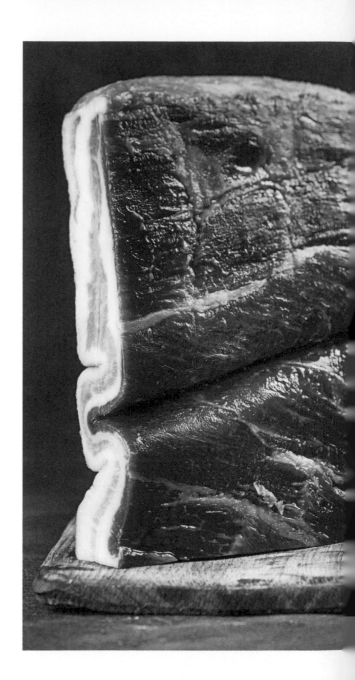

HOW TO CURE BACON

THE CURING PROCESS

Whichever you decide, don't discard the rind! It has many tasty uses. Here are some ideas for the using the rind:

* Stir it into traditional Southern recipes like pork and beans, cornbread, or collard greens to add extra flavor during cooking.

* Use it in traditional Italian recipes like *fagioli con le cotiche* (pork and beans) or *cotechinata* (a pork skin rolled up with bread crumbs and Italian seasonings, then baked). *Cotiche* means "pork skin" in Italian.

* Deep-fry it to make chicharrones, also referred to as pork cracklings or pork rinds. Pork cracklings have a bit of meat attached; pork rinds don't.

At Baconfreak.com, we've created a handy-dandy cure kit that has everything you need to cure your own bacon. If you want to purchase everything separately, here's what you will need:

* Five-pound pork belly
* Cure ingredients (see recipe on page 10)
* Large Ziploc® bag
* Meat thermometer
* Smoker and wood chips

Be sure to ask the butcher for a raw, or uncured, pork belly. You will need to start curing it within a couple days of bringing it home.

Bacon cure consists of three ingredients: salt, sugar, and pink curing salt. Pink curing salt is also called Prague Powder #1, Insta Cure #1, or Pink Curing Salt #1. Prague powder gets its name from the city of Prague which was once famous throughout Europe for its meatpacking industry. Pink curing salt contains 6 percent sodium nitrate and 94 percent table salt. It is recommended for meats that require short cures and will be cooked and eaten relatively quickly. The sodium nitrate prevents the growth of bacteria during the curing process and provides the characteristic flavor and pink color to the meat associated with curing. It also promotes the penetration of the salt evenly through the pork belly to prevent spoilage.

Pink curing salts purposely contain a dye that gives it a cotton candy color. This is so it won't be confused with regular table salt; pink curing salt can be toxic when not used at recommended levels. Also, do not confuse pink curing salt with Himalayan pink salt, which is a sea salt containing elements that give it its pink hue and is not suitable for curing meat. Pink curing salt can be purchased online. Lastly, do not confuse Prague Powder #1 with Prague Powder #2. Prague Powder #2 is used to cure meats that require a longer cure time of weeks to months, like hard salami and country hams.

Sugar is another important ingredient of the cure. The addition of sugar will balance out the saltiness. While many diets like the Whole30® diet and the Paleo™ diet recommend curing bacon without sugar, eliminating sugar from the cure will result in a much saltier bacon. If you want a completely sugar-free bacon, you can experiment with leaving it out, but be aware that your end product will be very, very salty. The actual amount of sugar per serving in the cured bacon is minimal. The salt is important because that draws out the moisture from the meat. Hence, the "dry-cure" method.

INGREDIENTS FOR THE CURE

- ½   cup salt
- ½   cup granulated sugar
- 2   teaspoons pink curing salt #1 or Prague powder #1

This recipe is suitable for curing a 5-pound pork belly. You will need to adjust the ratios, depending on the weight of your pork belly.

EXTRAS

In addition to these ingredients, you can also add a variety of herbs, spices, and other ingredients to the cure to "mix it up." Here are some suggestions:

* 5 smashed garlic cloves and 2 tablespoons of crushed black peppercorns
* ¼ cup honey and 2 tablespoons of BBQ seasoning
* ¼ cup maple syrup, 1 tablespoon cinnamon, and 1 teaspoon nutmeg

INSTRUCTIONS FOR DRY-CURED BACON IN SEVEN EASY STEPS

1 Mix the 3 cure ingredients together, adding in extra ingredients, if desired. If you will be removing the skin, do so at this time. Rub the cure evenly over every surface of the pork belly. Use the entire amount of the cure. Place the belly in a large, sturdy, sealable Ziploc bag, removing as much air as possible. Put the belly on a rimmed baking sheet or roasting pan, just in case the bag leaks. Place the pan on the bottom shelf of the refrigerator.

2 Turn the pork belly over once a day and give it a little love pat. After all, it'll soon be your own beloved homemade bacon! The belly needs to cure in the refrigerator for 7 days. You will notice that liquid is accumulating in the bag. This is normal. This means the salt is doing its job of removing any liquid from the meat. Way to go, salt! Turning the belly each day allows each side of the slab to have equal exposure to the liquid.

3 After 7 days, remove the belly from the refrigerator. It should feel firm, but still pliable. If it's too soft, it will need another day or two in the bag in the fridge. After the belly is sufficiently cured, give it a thorough rinse to remove any remaining cure. Pat the belly dry using paper towels or a dishcloth. Dry it thoroughly. Place it on a wire rack on a baking sheet, and place it back in the refrigerator. Leave it in overnight. This will help the smoke adhere to the meat through the formation of a pellicle. A pellicle is a dry, tacky surface on meat that helps to absorb the smoke.

4 Check the level of saltiness before smoking. Cut off a small portion of meat and fry it in a pan. When it's cooked, take a bit and see if it's excessively salty. If the level of salt is too high, soak the belly in cold water for a few hours and test it again. If it's acceptable, repeat the drying and formation of the pellicle from step 3. If you intend to use the bacon as an ingredient in a recipe or a soup, as opposed to eating it on its own, you may want it saltier than you would otherwise.

5 The smoking process is where the magic happens! Follow the manufacturer's instructions on your home smoker. We recommend good ol' hickory chips, but you can experiment with different wood chips, such as maplewood, applewood, pecanwood, or cherrywood. Cook the belly at 200°F until the internal temperature reaches 145°F. This should take 2–3 hours for a 5-pound belly.

6 Allow the freshly smoked slab to cool in the refrigerator for several hours or overnight, if you can wait that long! This will help the flavors set.

If you're refrigerating the belly overnight, wrap it tightly in plastic wrap.

7 If you left the rind on, remove it now. Get started slicing those strips! You can decide how thick or how thin you want them. That's part of the beauty of curing bacon at home. Handle your freshly cured bacon strips with care and cook over medium heat. Your homemade bacon will keep for 7 days in the fridge or up to 3 months in the freezer.

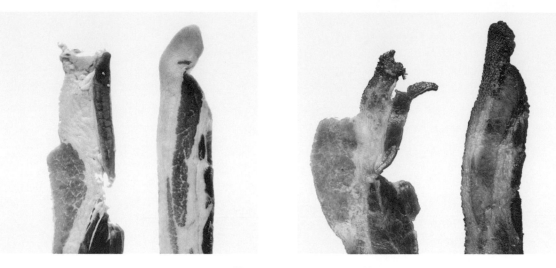

LEFT: **Wet-cured bacon.** RIGHT: **Dry-cured bacon.**

These three bacon strips were cooked in the skillet, oven, and microwave. Can you tell which is which? Left strip, microwave; middle strip, oven; right strip, skillet.

Bacon Basics

Now that you know so much about the dry-cure process, you'll understand why we recommend dry-cured bacon in our recipes. Dry-cured bacon results in thick, meaty slices that will impart the most flavor and texture. We also recommend cooking with high-quality, artisan bacon.

HOW TO COOK BACON

The best way to cook bacon is in the oven. It's the easiest way to cook bacon because you won't need multiple frying pans and you don't need to flip it repeatedly as it cooks. It's also the ideal method because the evenness of the oven temperature will ensure that the strips end up perfectly crispy and delicious. Cleanup is a cinch, too. This baking method depends on the thickness and quality of your bacon strips, so keep that in mind when you set the timer.

When it comes to bacon texture, the crispy versus chewy debate is as old as bacon itself. When eating bacon on its own, you may prefer a crispy texture. However, when cooking bacon for the purpose of adding it to a recipe where it will cook longer (like a frittata or mac & cheese), we recommend cooking it to a chewy texture. This is because the bacon will continue cooking in the dish. Oven cooking will ultimately give you the best control and allow you to cook your bacon exactly the way you want it.

Here are a few pointers to help you achieve the best-tasting, best-cooked bacon. These tips can be applied to any cooking method and will prevent the overcooking or burning of your precious meat candy.

1 Before cooking the bacon, let it sit at room temperature for 15 minutes. We know it sounds weird and kinda gross, but trust us. Room-temperature bacon means the fat will render out more quickly, and that helps the fat get crispy and decreases the likelihood of burning.

2 Do not preheat your oven or skillet. That's right. Never put bacon in a warm oven or a hot skillet. By putting the bacon in a cold oven or skillet, it will cook much more slowly, allowing more fat to be rendered out, which will increase your level of crispiness. It'll also help to avoid burning the meaty parts.

3 Do not overcrowd the bacon. Leaving an inch between the strips will also help the fat to render out and prevent the bacon from steaming, rather than baking or frying. Steamed bacon is floppy bacon, and you don't want that, do you? We didn't think so.

BACON BITS

The phrase *bringing home the bacon* originated in 1104 in the town of Dunmow in Essex, England. The church in Dunmow would award a "flitch," or a side of bacon, to any man who could honestly say that he had not argued with his wife for a year.

4 Keep an eye on it! Don't leave your precious bacon alone. Bacon can go from deliciously perfectly done to burnt and inedible in an instant. Be especially mindful of this if you're cooking bacon with sugar in it, like maple or apple cinnamon.

5 For safety reasons, the USDA recommends that cuts of pork be cooked to a temperature of at least 145°F.

6 Bacon grease is a prized commodity and can be used in different and delicious ways. If you are wondering what to do with your bacon grease after cooking, here are a few suggestions:

* Use it to fry up those green things called veggies.
* Use melted bacon fat when making homemade popcorn.
* Use it to grease the pan when making recipes like cornbread, biscuits, pancakes, and waffles.
* To store bacon grease for later use, drain it into a glass jar with a tight-fitting lid and store it in the refrigerator. Bacon grease will last for at least a month in the fridge when stored properly.

HOW TO COOK BACON IN THE OVEN

1 *Do not* preheat the oven.

2 Line a baking sheet with parchment paper. If you like, you can place a wire cooling rack on the baking sheet. This will let the fat render out as the grease runs off and will result in crispier bacon. You can also use a Pyrex® or casserole dish. Adding parchment paper is optional but will help with cleanup.

3 Put the bacon strips on the baking sheet, the cooling rack, or the baking dish. Place on the middle rack of the oven.

4 *Now* you can turn your oven to 375°F. If you are using a dark baking sheet, lower the temperature to 350°F. As the oven heats up, the bacon will cook at a gradually increasing temperature. This means it will cook all the way through without getting too crispy or burnt.

5 Check the bacon in about 12–14 minutes. Some types of bacon may take longer than others, depending upon the thickness of the cut. Extra-thick bacon could take up to 25 minutes. Depending on the distribution of heat in your oven, you may need to flip the strips halfway through cooking

BACON BITS

The BLT became popular in the 1950s when grocery stores were able to offer fresh lettuce and tomatoes year-round.

6 Let the bacon cook until it reaches your desired level of doneness. Remove the baking sheet from the oven and, using tongs or a fork, move the bacon to a plate lined with paper towels to absorb the remaining fat and grease. **7** What are you waiting for?? Pig out! (Pun obviously intended.)

HOW TO COOK BACON ON THE STOVETOP

So, you can't imagine cooking bacon any other way than on the stovetop. We get it. There's something nostalgic about frying bacon in a cast-iron skillet!

1 Lay the bacon strips in a nonstick frying pan or a seasoned skillet.

2 Turn on the heat to medium-low and cook the bacon until it starts to release its fat. Increase temperature to medium. Flip the strips halfway through cooking.

3 Continue cooking until each side is evenly cooked to your desired level of doneness (crispy versus chewy; it's a conundrum).

4 Transfer the cooked strips to a plate lined with paper towels to absorb the grease.

5 If you have more bacon to cook, drain the excess grease and continue cooking the remaining strips the same way.

HOW TO COOK BACON IN THE MICROWAVE

There are some foods that just don't microwave well, and bacon is one of them. It's very easy to overcook bacon in the microwave, and precious bacon is a terrible thing to waste. Yuck! Don't do it. Just don't.

HOW TO COOK FROZEN BACON

Got a hankerin' for some bacon and all you have is bacon that's been in the freezer? Not to worry! Just put it in a cold water bath and after 10–15 minutes, it'll thaw out and be ready to cook. Need chopped bacon for a recipe? Frozen bacon is actually much easier to chop than fresh bacon and won't stick together.

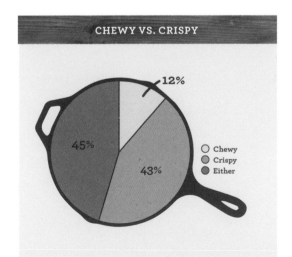

CHEWY VS. CRISPY

12%

45%

43%

○ Chewy
○ Crispy
● Either

HOW TO MAKE CANDIED BACON

There's bacon . . . and then there's candied bacon. Candied bacon is a one-two punch of sweet and salty that your palate will find irresistible. Candied bacon tastes amazing all on its own. Refer to these instructions when making recipes that require candied bacon:

1   cup light brown sugar
1   pound bacon

1 Place wire cooling racks in a shallow baking dish or jelly-roll pan, lined with aluminum foil. Spray with nonstick spray.

2 Dredge each slice of bacon in the brown sugar, or use your hands to coat both sides of the strips. Set each piece of coated bacon on the wire cooling rack.

3 Place the baking sheet in the oven, Then turn the temperature to 375°F. Bake for 15–20 minutes or until the bacon appears to be caramelized and somewhat crispy. Keep an eye on it, since the sugar can begin to burn when left in for too long.

4 Try to avoid eating all of it in one sitting. *We know. It's hard.*

HOW TO MAKE PORK RINDS

* Cut the skin into 2–3" strips.
* With a sharp knife, remove the fat from the strips of skin, being careful not to slice the skin. The more fat you are able to remove, the crispier the cracklings will be when fried.
* Place the strips of skin, fat side down, on wire racks in a baking pan, then place the pan in a preheated 250°F oven.
* Bake until the skin is dried out. This will ensure that they crisp up during frying.
* Deep-fry the skin in batches until crisp and puffy.
* After they are fried, you can flavor them with a variety of seasonings. Experiment with different combinations, like cinnamon sugar, cayenne pepper and lime zest, BBQ seasoning, or good ol' salt and pepper.
* Eat them all on their own, or add to recipes like Crackling Cornbread.

HOW TO MAKE A BACON WEAVE

A bacon weave is an invaluable asset in the kitchen. Use a bacon weave in a BLT or on a burger to ensure crispy, tasty bacon in every bite. It's easier to make a bacon weave with thin-cut bacon.

1 Begin by laying out 4–5 strips vertically on a baking sheet, making sure the strips are on the same level. Leave 1 strip's width between the strips.

2 Beginning on the left side, take a new strip of bacon and weave it through the other strips, alternating under and over, going under the first vertical strip of bacon. Repeat with another piece of bacon, only this time go *over* the first vertical strip.

3 As you weave, make sure there are no spaces between woven strips. You want a fairly tight weave that will hold together.

4 Once the weave is complete, place the baking sheet in the oven. Set the oven to 375°F and bake for 12–20 minutes, depending on the thickness of the bacon.

Bacon and Health

Bacon and *healthy* are two words that do not usually appear in the same sentence. Bacon lovers usually have a bacon naysayer in their life who likes to nag them about their "unhealthy" relationship with their One True Love. However, bacon is no longer the health horror it was once thought to be. In fact, the opposite is proving to be true. It's satisfying to know that bacon loves your body just as much as you love bacon!

Two major studies emerged during the 1980s, calling out dietary fat as the most crucial component of the American diet that needed to be changed in order to improve overall health. The suspected culprit was saturated fat, which raises LDL (the so-called "bad") cholesterol levels. But to simplify things for the general public, a reduction in *all* fats was called for.

During the 1990s, the "fat free" phenomenon really took off. Having two eggs for breakfast was considered horribly detrimental to your health, but scarfing down an entire sleeve of fat-free, double-fudge cookie bars was totally acceptable. Mmmkay . . .

Soon the USDA dietary guidelines recommended that people replace high-fat dairy and meat with more whole grains. The general message given off by the USDA, health-care professionals, and food companies was that "Fat is bad, carbs are good." So what did people do? They replaced milk, cheese, and high-fat meats with low-fat pasta, potatoes, and rice.

The no-fat diet backfired in a big, big way as

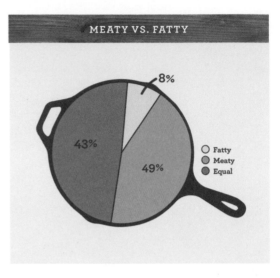

MEATY VS. FATTY

8%

43%

49%

○ Fatty
● Meaty
● Equal

the overemphasis on eliminating fat led to an overconsumption of carbohydrates and refined sugar. According to recent studies, the shift that occurred during the 1990s can be linked to an increase in obesity and diabetes that still plagues us as a nation today.

Today, health-care professionals and nutritionists recommend that people include healthy fats in their diet. Low-carb, high-fat diets are all the rage. The gluten-free trend seems here to stay. Wheat is "out" and fat is "in," which is great news for bacon fans. Diets like the Paleo diet, the Atkins diet, the Wheat Belly diet, and the Whole30® diet are gaining in popularity. These diets all have one thing in common: They eliminate whole grains and recommend the consumption of meat, bacon, olive oil, coconut oil, avocados, and nuts.

Here's what today's doctors and medical studies have to say on the matter of bacon's health benefits. Keep this list in mind when you're having breakfast with friends and they give you the stink eye for ordering extra bacon. And the next time Aunt Edna rolls her eyes because you've brought bacon-wrapped meatballs to the family potluck, rattle off some of these "reasons why bacon is healthy for you."

1. WE ♥ BACON AND BACON ♥ YOUR ♥

Dr. John Salerno is one of bacon's biggest proponents. Dr. Salerno is a world-renowned physician, with over fifteen years of clinical experience. Best known for his weight-loss treatments among patients and celebrities, he also specializes in bioidentical hormone

replacement therapy, vitamin therapy infusions, and anti-aging medicine. Dr. Salerno is the author of several books, including *Fight Fat with Fat, The Silver Cloud Diet,* and *The Salerno Solution.* An important component of his diet is the inclusion of healthy fat sources, including nuts, olives, avocados, and, yes, your beloved bacon.

Saturated fat is important in everyone's diet. Our brain cells and bodies need fat in order to thrive and function at optimal levels. Saturated fats are not the culprit when it comes to conditions such as heart disease and high cholesterol, and recent studies have shown that increasing your intake of saturated fat actually lowers your risk of heart disease, high cholesterol, and chronic degenerative diseases. Many who suffer from Parkinson's, Alzheimer's, epilepsy, multiple sclerosis, and ALS are finding significant relief by following a high-fat, low-carb diet.

Bacon also contains essential omega-3 fatty acids, which the body can't produce on its own and must be obtained through diet. According to Dr. Salerno, studies have shown that pasture-raised, grass-fed, nitrate-free bacon contains as much, and sometimes more, omega-3 fatty acids than most fish. He adds that, although some fish contain their fair share of omega-3s, they also have another not-so-good quality—unsafe levels of mercury and heavy metals. This makes some omega-3 supplements less healthy than previously considered.

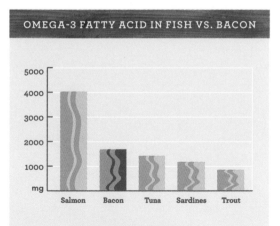

OMEGA-3 FATTY ACID IN FISH VS. BACON

5000
4000
3000
2000
1000
mg

Salmon   Bacon   Tuna   Sardines   Trout

*Amounts are based on a 3oz serving of meat. All information is from nutritiondata.com.

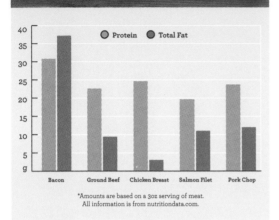

PROTEIN/FAT IN BACON VS. OTHER MEAT

● Protein ● Total Fat

*Amounts are based on a 3oz serving of meat.
All information is from nutritiondata.com.

2. PORK-POWERED PROTEIN

Protein is a vital component of the human diet. Every cell in your body contains a protein molecule. Your body uses protein to make tissues, enzymes, hormones, muscles, cartilage, skin, and blood. Protein is a macronutrient (like fat and carbohydrates), which means that the body needs relatively large amounts of it to ensure optimal health. The protein found in bacon contains all the necessary amino acids that are vital to maintaining a fully functioning, healthy body. Protein also boosts and maintains energy levels, and doesn't fill you up with empty calories that result in a roller-coaster ride of spiking blood sugar levels.

3. FLUSHING FAT WITH FLAVORFUL FLESH

The fat found in bacon helps to satiate our appetite, which can promote weight loss; boost

metabolism; and build lean, strong muscles. Fats are now an important component of modern "diets" like the Paleo diet, the Atkins diet, and the Fight Fat with Fat diet. Bacon has less total fat, saturated fat, and cholesterol per serving than many popular cuts of beef, chicken, and pork.

4. BACON'S BRAIN-BUILDING BASICS

Bacon is chock-full of a very important nutrient called choline, which helps improve long-term and short-term memory, attention, and memory processes. In university studies, it has been proven that people who get enough choline in their diets perform better on memory tests. Choline has even been shown to ward off the effects of Alzheimer's and other chronic mental impairments. Choline is a precursor to the brain

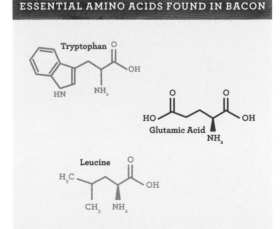

ESSENTIAL AMINO ACIDS FOUND IN BACON

Tryptophan

Glutamic Acid

Leucine

chemical acetylcholine, which plays a vital role in cognitive functions. Low acetylcholine levels are associated with Alzheimer's disease.

5. "PIG OUT" ON ESSENTIAL VITAMINS AND MINERALS

Bacon contains essential vitamins, minerals, and antioxidants, like zinc, phosphorous, iron, magnesium, selenium, and many of the B vitamins, including B_1 (thiamine), B_2 (riboflavin), B_3 (niacin), B_6 (pyridoxine), and B_{12} (cyanocobalamin). These vitamins and minerals are essential for proper body function.

6. EFFECTIVE MOOD ELEVATOR

When you cook bacon, you feel relaxed. When you smell it cooking, you feel happy and excited. When you eat a piece of bacon, you feel a wide range of positive emotions. That's because bacon has an effect on the brain that is similar to the effect that cocaine has on it. Yes, it's true. Bacon is similar to cocaine in that when you eat it, the pleasure centers in the brain are overloaded. Bacon is a natural mood elevator.

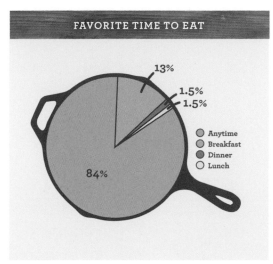

FAVORITE TIME TO EAT

13%
1.5%
1.5%
84%

- Anytime
- Breakfast
- Dinner
- Lunch

7. NITRATES AND NITRITES: NOW NONISSUES

Bacon has been maligned for being a member of the cured-meat family. Older studies suggested that there was a link between eating cured meats and certain types of cancer. However, the original study on nitrates and cancer risk has since been discredited. If you want to avoid nitrates, you'll have to avoid a lot of other foods, not just bacon. For example, celery, lettuce, spinach, and beets all have high nitrate content, and to say that those are unhealthy is downright silly.

8. BACON MAKES VEGGIES BETTER

Adding bacon makes those icky foods that people call "vegetables" so much better! Even something as simple as tossing veggies

BACON BITS

A recent weight-loss study found that women who added bacon to their breakfast felt less hungry at lunchtime and lost the same amount of weight as women who had no protein at breakfast.

in bacon fat before cooking them will vastly improve their flavor and appeal. For someone who doesn't like veggies, try adding bacon to get those recommended daily servings of veggies in. After all, bacon *is* a vegetable!

9. BACON'S BLOOD-BALANCING BOUNTY

Several studies have shown that including bacon as a regular, moderate part of one's diet does not negatively affect blood pressure or blood sugar levels. In fact, when bacon is consumed in moderation, it can be effective at lowering blood pressure; in preventing or alleviating the effects of diabetes; and in preventing heart disease, heart attacks, and strokes.

10. LONG LIVE LONGEVITY

We've saved the best for last. You won't need any more proof of bacon's health benefits when you hear about Pearl Cantrell and Susannah Mushatt Jones. Pearl Cantrell made headlines on her 105th birthday, when she claimed that eating bacon was the key to her longevity. Cantrell ate two pieces of bacon a day for breakfast and sometimes at lunch. Susannah Mushatt Jones celebrated her 116th birthday in 2015, becoming the world's oldest person. Jones's daily breakfast consisted of bacon, eggs, and grits. A sign in her kitchen read "Bacon Makes Everything Better."

What Is Your Favorite Bacon Pairing?

BACON AND. . .

ANYTHING STEAK VODKA MUSHROOMS
COFFEE CHOCOLATE GRITS CORNBREAD
HAMBURGERS BOURBON MAPLE SYRUP
ICE CREAM BLUE CHEESE COFFEE BISCUITS BLT
SCALLOPS APPLE PIE PIZZA SHRIMP
PANCAKES BREAD TOMATOES
HAM BEER BRUSSELS SPROUTS CHICKEN WAFFLES
MEATLOAF CUPCAKES
BEANS CHEESE BACON DOUGHNUTS
CARAMEL WHISKEY
EGGS TOAST BLOODY MARY
PEANUT BUTTER
PASTA AVOCADO ASPARAGUS
POTATOES JALAPEÑOS MAC AND CHEESE

THE
RECIPES

Bacon:
It's What's
for Brunch

Bacon
Apple Cider

We combined traditional mulling spices with a hint of bacon flavor
to create a smoky apple cider that's perfect for any holiday celebrations.
Make this cider a day ahead for a stronger bacon flavor and aroma.

WE RECOMMEND Baby Bubba's Apple
Cinnamon Bacon
MAKES approximately 6 cups
PREP TIME 5 minutes
COOK TIME 35 minutes
TOTAL TIME 40 minutes

  5 cups apple juice
  1 cup water
  ¼ cup real maple syrup
  2 strips bacon
  2 cinnamon sticks
  1 teaspoon whole cloves
     peel of 1 orange

1 Bring apple juice, water, and maple syrup to a boil in a large saucepan. While the juice is heating, cook bacon in a skillet until just cooked through and drain on paper towels to absorb the excess grease. Press a paper towel into the bacon to absorb as much grease as possible.

2 Add the cinnamon, cloves, orange peel, and bacon to the juice and simmer over low heat for about 30 minutes. Remove from heat and strain out the spices, orange peel, and bacon. Serve immediately or store it in the fridge overnight for optimal bacon flavor infusion. Reheat before serving.

Bacon Strawberry Hazelnut Spread Crepes

Is this breakfast or is it dessert? Why not have dessert for breakfast!
Sweeten your weekend brunch routine with these light, airy crepes
that taste as if they're straight from a Parisian café.

WE RECOMMEND Boss Hog Hickory-Smoked Bacon

DRINK PAIRING Bring out the hazelnut flavors with an Irish Hazelnut Cream cocktail. Mix equal parts Irish whiskey with hazelnut liqueur and top with a healthy dollop of whipped cream.

MAKES Four 12" crepes

PREP TIME 10 minutes

COOK TIME 15 minutes

TOTAL TIME 25 minutes

- 1 cup all-purpose flour
- 2 eggs
- ½ cup whole milk
- ½ cup water
- ¼ teaspoon of salt
- 1 tablespoon bacon grease, melted
- 1 13-oz jar hazelnut spread
- 1 cup ripe strawberries, sliced
- 16 strips bacon, cooked
- powdered sugar

1 Preheat oven to 200°F.

2 Whisk the flour and eggs together in a mixing bowl. Gradually stir in the milk and water. Mix in the salt and bacon grease, whisking until smooth.

3 Heat a greased crepe pan or large skillet over medium-high heat. Pour ½ cup of batter on the griddle, tilting the pan so that the batter evenly coats its surface.

4 Cook for about 2 minutes until the crepe is lightly browned on the bottom. Loosen with a spatula, then carefully flip the crepe. Allow the other side to cook for about 2 minutes. Carefully remove the crepe and repeat with remaining batter. Keep cooked crepes on a baking sheet in the warmed oven.

5 To assemble, add a generous amount of hazelnut spread to each crepe and spread evenly with a knife. Add strawberries and 4 strips of cooked bacon to each crepe. Roll the crepe or fold it in quarters, then dust with powdered sugar. Serve warm.

BACON FREAK

Bacon Weave
Chorizo Breakfast Burrito

LEVEL OF
DIFFICULTY

This breakfast burrito is a carnivore's dream come true. The tomato and avocado "salsa" balances out the heavy, meaty flavors and tones down the spiciness of the chorizo. For those who want even more spiciness, add some liberal doses of your favorite bacon-flavored hot sauce.

WE RECOMMEND Bourbon Street Cajun Bacon

DRINK PAIRING Who says you can't have beer for breakfast? Pair this with your favorite Mexican pilsner or lager, like Negra Modelo or Pacifico.

MAKES 1 burrito

PREP TIME 10 minutes

COOK TIME 35–40 minutes

TOTAL TIME 45–50 minutes

- 1 10–12-strip bacon weave, cooked (see page 18)
- ¼ avocado, diced
- ¼ tomato, diced
- 2 tablespoons onion, diced
- 1 tablespoon fresh cilantro
  salt and pepper
- ¼ cup chorizo
- 2 eggs, beaten
- 1 cup jack cheese, shredded
- 1 12" tortilla

1 Prepare the bacon weave by weaving 10–12 strips of bacon together. Carefully place the weave on a parchment-lined baking sheet and bake at 375°F for 25–30 minutes until bacon starts to crisp. Remove from oven and drain on paper towels.

2 In a small bowl, combine avocado, tomato, onion, cilantro, salt, and pepper to taste. Stir until well combined. Refrigerate until ready to use.

3 Cook the chorizo in a skillet over medium heat. When the chorizo is cooked, add the beaten eggs and scramble together. Cook until eggs are cooked through. Add cheese to skillet and remove from heat.

4 To assemble, lay the bacon weave on top of the tortilla. Spoon the egg mixture in a line in the center of the bacon weave, then top with avocado/tomato mixture and roll into the shape of a burrito. Serve immediately with hot sauce or your favorite salsa.

Bacon Pancake Sausage Stackers

To make these stackers more savory and spicy, use spicy bacon. To make them sweeter, use maple-cured bacon. This is a fun recipe to make with kids, and kids and adults alike will enjoy building their own breakfast.

WE RECOMMEND Bourbon Street Cajun Bacon

DRINK PAIRING Maple beer, with a hint of sweet and smoky flavor, is the perfect complement to maple syrup and smoky bacon and sausage.

MAKES 4 stackers

PREP TIME 15 minutes

COOK TIME 20 minutes

TOTAL TIME 35 minutes

PANCAKES

- 1 cup all-purpose flour
- 1 tablespoon sugar
- 1 teaspoon baking powder
- ½ teaspoon baking soda
- ½ teaspoon salt
- 1 egg
- 1 cup buttermilk
- 2 strips bacon, cooked and chopped
- 2 tablespoons unsalted butter, melted
- 1 tablespoons maple syrup
- ½ teaspoon vanilla extract

STACKERS

- 8 ounces ground Italian sausage
- 8 strips of bacon, cooked and cut in half
  pure maple syrup (optional)
  whipped cream (optional)

1 Preheat oven to 200°F.

2 For the pancakes, combine in a large bowl the flour, sugar, baking powder, baking soda, and salt. In a separate bowl, beat the egg until frothy. Add in buttermilk, bacon bits, melted butter, maple syrup, and vanilla. Mix into the dry ingredients until just combined, being careful not to overmix the batter.

3 Heat a greased griddle over medium heat. Pour 2–3 tablespoons of batter onto the griddle to make 4" pancakes. Cook until the batter is set and tiny bubbles appear on the top, about 1–2 minutes. Flip the pancakes and cook until golden, about 1 more minute. Place cooked pancakes on a baking sheet in the warm oven. Repeat with remaining batter until you have 16 pancakes.

4 For the stackers, divide the Italian sausage into 4 round patties. Cook in a skillet over medium-high heat until meat is cooked through and browned on the outside. Remove from heat.

5 To assemble, layer as follows: 1 pancake, 2 bacon halves, 1 pancake, 1 sausage patty, 1 pancake, 2 bacon halves, 1 pancake. Top with a generous amount of pure maple syrup and a large dollop of whipped cream, if desired. Serve immediately.

Mocha Latte Bacon Pancakes

Get your caffeine, chocolate, and bacon fix in with every bite of these velvety pancakes. The coffee, chocolate, and bacon flavors complement each other well and are perfectly balanced. Make them either more sweet or more savory with your topping choices.

WE RECOMMEND Bourbon Street Vanilla Bourbon Bacon

DRINK PAIRING A robust stout with chocolate and coffee notes will make those flavors stand up and sing. Try a Young's Double Chocolate Stout, Kona Brewing Co. Pipeline Porter, or Sierra Nevada Coffee Stout.

MAKES Ten–twelve 5" pancakes

PREP TIME 20 minutes

COOK TIME 15 minutes

TOTAL TIME 35 minutes

- 1 cup all-purpose flour
- ¼ cup sugar
- 1 teaspoon baking powder
- ½ teaspoon baking soda
- 1 tablespoon espresso powder
- ¼ cup cocoa powder
- 1 egg
- ½ cup buttermilk
- ½ cup coffee, brewed
- 1 tablespoon bacon fat, melted
- ¼ cup dark chocolate chips
- 8 ounces bacon, cooked and chopped

1 Preheat oven to 175–200°F.

2 In a large bowl, combine the flour, sugar, baking powder, baking soda, espresso powder, and cocoa powder. In another large bowl, combine the egg, buttermilk, brewed coffee, and melted bacon fat. Add the liquid ingredients to the dry ingredients and stir until combined. Stir in the chocolate chips and bacon.

3 Heat a greased skillet or frying pan over medium heat. Pour in enough batter to make a 5" pancake. When the uncooked side of each pancake starts to bubble, flip the pancake and continue cooking until medium brown, about 1 minute. Repeat until all the batter is used, keeping the cooked pancakes on a baking sheet in the warmed oven.

Bacon
Bloody Mary
Biscuits and Gravy

Bacon has been proven to be an excellent hangover remedy. We took this factoid a step further to create this recipe—the ultimate hangover relief! Prepare everything on New Year's Eve Day, and then on New Year's Day the only heavy machinery you'll need to operate is your microwave and toaster oven.

WE RECOMMEND Swine King Garlic Paprika Bacon

DRINK PAIRING Mix up a classic Bloody Mary cocktail, of course!

MAKES 4 servings

PREP TIME 15 minutes

COOK TIME 25 minutes

TOTAL TIME 40 minutes

BISCUITS

- 1 cup unbleached all-purpose flour, plus more for dusting the board
- ⅛ teaspoon baking soda
- ½ tablespoon baking powder
- ½ teaspoon kosher salt
- 3 tablespoons unsalted butter, very cold
- ½ cup buttermilk (more if needed)

BLOODY MARY SAUCE

- 3 ounces ketchup
- 1 tablespoon brown sugar
- 1 teaspoon fresh lemon juice
- 1½ teaspoons horseradish
- 2 tablespoons water
- 1 tablespoon distilled vinegar
- ¼ teaspoon celery salt
- ¼ teaspoon cayenne pepper
- ¼ teaspoon garlic powder
- 1 teaspoon Worcestershire sauce
- ½ tablespoon cayenne hot sauce
- 1 slice bacon, cooked and chopped salt and pepper to taste

GRAVY

- 1 pound of bacon, divided
- 1 tablespoon all-purpose flour
- 1 cup milk, or as needed pepper to taste
- 1 teaspoon cayenne pepper

SANDWICH ASSEMBLY

- 4 eggs

LEVEL OF DIFFICULTY

1 Preheat the oven to 450°F.

2 Combine flour, baking soda, baking powder, and salt in a large bowl. Cut the butter into the flour until it resembles coarse meal. Add the buttermilk and mix until just combined. The dough should be very wet, so add a bit more buttermilk if it's too dry.

3 Gently pat the dough out to a ½" thickness. Fold the dough 4–5 times and gently press the dough down to a 1" thickness. Cut into quarters and form each piece into a biscuit shape. Place the biscuits on a parchment-lined baking sheet so their sides are touching. Bake for 10–12 minutes until they are a light-golden brown. Cool on a cooling rack.

4 While the biscuits are baking, prepare the Bloody Mary sauce by whisking all ingredients together until smooth. Refrigerate until ready to serve.

5 For the gravy, cook 5 pieces of bacon until crispy and set aside. Chop the remaining bacon and cook in a large skillet until crispy. Remove the cooked bacon, reserving all the grease. Heat the grease over medium-high heat. Gradually whisk in 1 tablespoon of flour and cook for 1 minute until smooth. Whisk in the milk and cook until thickened; do not let the milk boil. If the gravy is too thick, add a little more milk. Stir in the chopped bacon, pepper, and cayenne pepper. Remove from heat and set aside.

6 Fry the eggs over medium heat to your desired doneness. While the eggs are cooking, cut the biscuits in half and place on a plate. Top both halves with bacon gravy and 1 slice of bacon. When the eggs are done, place 1 egg on top of each serving, followed by a spoonful of bacon Bloody Mary sauce. Serve immediately.

Elvis Waffles

A peanut butter, banana, and bacon sandwich is named after the "King" because of his renowned fondness for them. We think Elvis would definitely approve of these delicious waffles. The key to getting light and fluffy waffles is not to overmix the batter.

WE RECOMMEND Boss Hog Hickory-Smoked Maple Bacon

DRINK PAIRING Boss Hog's Maple Bacon Coffee, spiked with your favorite booze

MAKES 5 waffles

PREP TIME 25 minutes

COOK TIME 15 minutes

TOTAL TIME 40 minutes

WAFFLES

- 2 cups all-purpose flour
- 2 tablespoons sugar
- 2 teaspoons baking powder
- 1 teaspoon baking soda
- ¾ teaspoon salt
- 1 teaspoon cinnamon
- 2 cups buttermilk
- 6 tablespoons unsalted butter, softened
- 2 large eggs
- ⅓ cup creamy peanut butter
- ½ cup bacon, cooked and chopped

TOPPING

- 2 ripe bananas, sliced
- ¼ cup honey
- 2 tablespoons peanut butter
- ½ cup bacon, cooked and chopped

1 Preheat oven to 200°F and preheat waffle iron according to manufacturer's instructions.

2 In a large bowl, whisk the flour, sugar, baking powder, baking soda, salt and cinnamon together. In another bowl, whisk the buttermilk, butter, eggs, and peanut butter together. Mix the dry ingredients into the wet ingredients until just combined, then gently fold in the cooked, chopped bacon.

3 Pour about ½ cup of batter onto a lightly greased waffle iron. Cook the waffles until they are cooked through and golden, about 3 minutes. Transfer the waffles to a baking sheet in the oven to keep them warm. Repeat steps 1–3 with the remaining batter.

4 In a large skillet, sauté the sliced bananas until browned. In a separate bowl, combine the honey and peanut butter. Fold in the bananas and chopped bacon. Serve on top of the cooked waffles and add a drizzle of honey, if desired.

Bacon Orange Marmalade Champagne Muffins

These delectable muffins are an elegant addition to Sunday brunch. The homemade marmalade has a wonderful flavor that balances sweet, smoky, and slightly tangy remarkably well.

WE RECOMMEND Rita Hogsworth Maplewood Bacon
DRINK PAIRING Champagne. Duh!
MAKES 12 muffins
PREP TIME 15 minutes
COOK TIME 15–20 minutes
TOTAL TIME 30–35 minutes

BACON ORANGE MARMALADE
- 6 strips bacon, roughly chopped
- 1 orange, peeled and chopped
- 2 tablespoons orange peel, chopped
- 1 cup champagne
- 1 teaspoon ground cinnamon
- ½ teaspoon ground cloves
- 1 cup sugar

MUFFINS
- 2½ cups all-purpose flour
- ½ cup sugar
- 4 teaspoons baking powder
- ½ teaspoon salt
- 1 stick (½ cup) melted butter
- 2 large eggs, at room temperature
- 1 teaspoon vanilla extract
- 1 cup champagne
- ¼ cup bacon bits

1 For the bacon orange marmalade, cook bacon in a medium saucepan until fat renders out and bacon begins to crisp. Add the orange, orange peel, champagne, and spices to the bacon. Bring to a boil and stir in the sugar. Simmer for 20 minutes then process in a blender until smooth. Transfer to a jar or an airtight container.

2 For the muffins, combine flour, sugar, baking powder, and salt in a large mixing bowl. In a separate small bowl, whisk the melted butter, eggs, and vanilla together. Lightly fold the wet ingredients into the dry ingredients, then stir in the champagne and bacon bits until everything is just combined.

3 Divide batter evenly into 12 cups of a greased muffin tin and bake for 15–18 minutes until light golden brown. Cool slightly and serve with a spoonful of marmalade on each muffin.

Boozy Candied Bacon

This recipe can be recreated with your favorite booze! Get creative with your toppings or, if you don't want to think too hard, we've got some fun suggestions below.

WE RECOMMEND Boss Hog Hickory-Smoked Bacon

MAKES 1 pound

PREP TIME 15 minutes

COOK TIME 15–20 minutes

REST TIME 6–8 hours

TOTAL TIME 6–8 hours

1 cup of your favorite booze
1 pound bacon
   brown or granulated sugar

1 Separate the bacon into strips. Lay each strip in a shallow baking dish or bowl. Add enough alcohol so the bacon is entirely covered. Cover with plastic wrap and refrigerate for 6–8 hours.

2 Remove bacon from fridge and discard the alcohol. Do not drink it! Pat each piece of bacon dry using a clean dishrag. Rub sugar lightly on both sides of each piece of bacon, and place pieces on a parchment-lined baking sheet.

3 Place the baking sheet in the oven, then heat to 375°F. Bake for 15–17 minutes, checking frequently so the bacon doesn't burn, flipping once if needed.

RECIPE SUGGESTIONS

Bourbon Candied Bacon

1 pound bacon
1 cup bourbon
¼–⅓ cup granulated sugar

Cadillac Margarita Bacon

1 pound bacon
¾ cup tequila
¼ cup orange juice
   juice of 1 lime
⅓–½ cup brown sugar
   zest of 1 lime

Mudslide Bacon

1 pound bacon
⅓ cup whipped cream vodka
⅓ cup coffee liqueur
⅓ cup Irish cream
¼–⅓ cup granulated sugar
   chocolate sauce (optional)

Cornish Bacon Pasties

Variations of the Cornish pasty can be found in many countries and cultures. Because who doesn't love a hearty, handheld pie made with a flaky crust that is stuffed with meat, cheese, and potatoes? It's the ultimate comfort food, no matter what you call it.

WE RECOMMEND Swine King Paprika Garlic or Firecracker Chili Bacon

DRINK PAIRING Serve with a traditional English cocktail, like a Pimm's Cup: a mix of Pimm's No. 1 gin and either ginger ale, lemonade, or lemon-lime soda, served in a glass with orange, lemon, or cucumber slices.

MAKES 6–8 pasties
PREP TIME 15 minutes
COOK TIME 40 minutes
REST TIME 30 minutes
TOTAL TIME 1 hour, 25 minutes

CRUST

2¼ cups all-purpose flour
½ teaspoon salt
3 ounces cold, unsalted butter, cut into pieces
3 ounces cold lard or vegetable shortening, cut into pieces
4–6 tablespoons water

FILLING

6 ounces mild cheddar cheese, shredded and divided
1 pound bacon, lightly cooked and chopped
½ white onion, finely chopped
1 small russet potato, cut into ¼" chunks
¼ teaspoon pepper
1–2 tablespoons hot sauce (optional)
1 egg
1 tablespoon water

1 For the crust, sift the flour and salt into a large bowl. Cut the butter and lard into the dry ingredients until the mixture resembles fine crumbs. Quickly mix the water into the flour mixture until it just comes together to form a dough. Briefly knead until the dough is smooth with no cracks; do not overwork the dough. Press into a flattened disk and wrap in plastic. Refrigerate for at least 30 minutes.

2 In a mixing bowl, combine 4 ounces of the cheese, chopped bacon, onion, potato, pepper, and optional hot sauce until thoroughly combined. Set aside.

3 Preheat the oven to 400°F.

4 Remove the dough from the refrigerator and the plastic rap. Allow to soften slightly and roll out to ¼" thickness on a floured surface. Using a small plate as your template, cut out 6–8 6" rounds. Gather the remaining scraps and roll out if needed. Place on a parchment-lined baking sheet.

5 Spoon about ¼ cup of the filling in the center of 1 dough round. Beat 1 egg with 1 tablespoon of water and brush it over the edges of the dough. Bring the unfilled side over the filled side so that the edges meet. Press the edges together to seal and then crimp, using your fingers or a fork. Repeat with the remaining rounds.

6 Brush the tops of the pasties with the remaining egg wash and then cut 1–2 slits into the top of each pie. Bake for 20 minutes until the crust is golden brown around the edges. Reduce the heat to 350°F. Sprinkle the remaining cheese on top of the pies and continue to bake until golden brown and the cheese is melted, about 5 more minutes. Cool for 15 minutes before serving.

CHAPTER 4

Comfort Food Mains and Sides

Bacon-Wrapped Fried Ravioli

There's nothing better than bacon, but these homemade ravioli come pretty close. They can be bacon-wrapped and deep-fried for an over-the-top appetizer that is guaranteed to impress your guests. Or serve them as a main dish with a pesto or brown butter sauce.

WE RECOMMEND Giovanni's
Delicioso Oregano Parmesan Bacon
DRINK PAIRING *Roberto Rogness
(see page 138) Recommends*
This screams for Sangiovese,
Montepulciano, or, if you are really
getting in the Italian groove, a dry
Lambrusco.

MAKES 28–32 ravioli
PREP TIME 30 minutes
COOK TIME 15 minutes
REST TIME 30 minutes
TOTAL TIME 1 hour, 15 minutes

DOUGH

- 3 cups all-purpose flour
- 3 eggs
- 6 tablespoons water
- 1 teaspoon olive oil

FILLING

- 7 ounces ricotta cheese
- 8 ounces mozzarella cheese, shredded
- ½ cup bacon, cooked and chopped
- 1 egg yolk, lightly beaten
- 2 teaspoons minced fresh basil
- 1 teaspoon minced fresh parsley
- ¼ teaspoon minced garlic

COATING

- 14–16 bacon strips
- oil for frying
- 2 cups Italian breadcrumbs
- 1 cup buttermilk

1 Stretch each piece of bacon before cookng to ensure that it will fit around the ravioli.

2 To make the dough, place flour in a large bowl and make a well in the center. Whisk together the eggs, water, and oil, then pour into the well. Mix together until the dough forms a ball. On a floured surface, knead the dough for 5–7 minutes until smooth. If the dough is sticky, add additional flour. Cover the dough and let it rest for 30 minutes.

3 Prepare the filling by mixing the ricotta, mozzarella, chopped bacon, egg yolk, basil, parsley, and garlic in a medium bowl until well combined. Refrigerate covered until ready to use.

4 Divide the dough in half. Roll the dough out on a floured surface until very thin, about ¹⁄₁₆". Drop 1 teaspoon of filling 1" apart over half of the pasta sheet, then brush around the filling with water to moisten the dough. Carefully fold the other half of the dough so it covers the filling. Cut into squares and seal the edges tightly. Repeat with the remaining dough and filling.

5 Add the ravioli to a pot of gently simmering, salted water for 5 minutes. Drain and let cool 1–2 minutes. Wrap ½ strip of bacon around the ravioli, securing with a toothpick.

6 In a large skillet, heat 1" of oil over medium-high heat. Fill 1 shallow bowl with breadcrumbs, and 1 with buttermilk. Dip the ravioli in buttermilk, letting any excess drip off, and then dredge the ravioli in the breadcrumbs. Fry in small batches for 1–2 minutes, turning once, until golden brown. Use a slotted spoon to transfer to a plate lined with paper towels to drain. Remove toothpick. Once all the ravioli are cooked, serve with your choice of sauce.

Bacon is Gouda Scalloped Potatoes

We used smoky gouda cheese and smoked paprika to perfectly complement the smokiness of bacon in this rich scalloped potato recipe. It's impossible to eat only one serving of these sinfully decadent potatoes. This recipe can be prepped the day before. Simply pop 'em in the oven 30 minutes before dinnertime.

WE RECOMMEND Swine King Paprika Garlic Bacon

DRINK FAIRING A crisp, dry martini will cut the richness of these creamy, cheesy potatoes.

MAKES 10–12 servings
PREP TIME 15 minutes
COOK TIME 1 hour, 30 minutes
TOTAL TIME 1 hour, 45 minutes

- 1 pound bacon
- 4 tablespoons reserved bacon grease
- 3 tablespoons all-purpose flour
- 1 teaspoon salt
- ½ teaspoon pepper
- 2½ cups milk
- 1 cup smoked gouda, shredded (more for topping, if desired)
- Pinch of nutmeg
- ½ teaspoon smoked paprika
- 5 large russet potatoes, thinly sliced
- ½ sweet onion, thinly sliced

1 Preheat oven to 400°F. Butter a 9" x 13" casserole dish.

2 In a large skillet, fry the bacon until cooked but not crispy, about 7–10 minutes. Transfer bacon to paper towels to drain, reserving 4 tablespoons of bacon grease in the pan. Chop up the bacon.

3 Heat the bacon grease over medium-high heat, then mix in the flour, salt, and pepper and whisk continuously for 1 minute. Stir in the milk in ½ cup increments, whisking to avoid lumps. Once all the milk is added, continue to cook over low-medium heat until the roux has thickened, stirring constantly.

4 Stir in the cheese, nutmeg, and paprika, and stir until the cheese is melted, about 1 minute.

5 Layer half the potatoes on the bottom of the prepared casserole dish. Top with the sliced onion, half of the cheese sauce, and half of the bacon. Add the remaining potatoes, followed by the remaining cheese sauce and bacon.

6 Cover the casserole dish with foil and bake for 1 hour. Remove the foil, then cook for another 30 minutes. Add more shredded cheese during the last 30 minutes of cooking, if desired.

Fennel Black Pepper Bacon Spread and Sausage Stuffing

This recipe is from Skillet Street Food in Seattle, Washington (www.skilletstreetfood.com). It uses Skillet Street's Fennel Black Pepper Bacon Spread, an aromatic, savory, and flavorful bacon condiment. Made with Italian sausage, fresh herbs, and cremini mushrooms, this will be a big hit with friends and family on Thanksgiving.

DRINK PAIRING Pair this savory stuffing recipe with your favorite Thanksgiving Day dinner wine.

MAKES 6 servings

PREP TIME 15 minutes

COOK TIME 40 minutes

TOTAL TIME 55 minutes

- 1 large onion, chopped
- ¾ cup Fennel Black Pepper Bacon Spread
- 3 garlic cloves, finely chopped
- 8 ounces Italian sausage
- 2 tablespoons chopped fresh Italian parsley
- 1 tablespoon chopped fresh thyme
- ¼ cup dry white wine
- 1 stick (½ cup) butter, diced
- ¾ cup chicken broth
- 1 16-ounce loaf of bread, cubed
- 8 ounces cremini mushrooms, sliced
- salt and pepper to taste
- 1 large egg, beaten

1 Preheat the oven to 350°F.

2 Combine the onions and bacon spread in a saucepan; sauté until tender, about 4 minutes. Add the garlic and sauté until fragrant, about 30 seconds. Add the sausage, parsley, and thyme then cook until the sausage browns, about 4 minutes. Add mushrooms until just browned. Add the wine and bring to a simmer. Melt in the butter, then remove from the heat and stir in the broth.

3 Place bread cubes in a large bowl then add the sausage mixture and toss thoroughly. Season the stuffing to taste with salt and pepper. Mix in the beaten egg. Transfer the stuffing to a 13" x 9" x 2" baking dish. Cover with foil and bake for 25 minutes. Uncover and bake another 15 minutes until the top begins to brown.

Apple Bacon Chicken Pies

Made with crispy, tart apples and savory Swiss cheese, these mini-pies are topped with a bacon weave to show off the star ingredient.

~~~~~~

WE RECOMMEND Caribbean Dream Bacon

DRINK PAIRING A hard cider with a hint of sweetness, like Angry Orchard's Crisp Apple Cider

MAKES 4 servings

PREP TIME 20 minutes

COOK TIME 45 minutes

TOTAL TIME 1 hour, 5 minutes

CHEESE SAUCE

- 1 tablespoon butter
- 2 tablespoons flour
- 1¼ cups 2 percent milk, at room temperature
- ¾ cup Swiss cheese
- ¼ teaspoon sage
- salt and pepper to taste

PIES

- 4 mini–bacon weaves
- 1 medium red onion, thinly sliced
- 2 tablespoons bacon grease
- 2 chicken breasts, cooked and shredded
- salt and pepper to taste
- ¼ teaspoon ground sage
- 2 Gala apples, peeled and sliced
- ½ cup dried cranberries
- ½ cup bacon, cooked and chopped

1 Form a 6" x 6" bacon weave (see page 18) and cook until just starting to crisp, about 20 minutes. Then carefully transfer it to paper towels to drain. Reserve the bacon grease.

2 For the cheese sauce, melt butter in a small saucepan over medium heat. Stir in the flour and cook until smooth. Slowly add the milk, stirring until combined. Once it starts to bubble, reduce heat, add cheese and sage, and then cook until the cheese is melted. Add salt and pepper to taste.

3 Preheat oven to 425°F.

4 For the pies, sauté the onions with 2 tablespoons of bacon grease in a large pan until transparent. Add chicken, salt, pepper, and sage. Cook for 5 minutes and set aside.

5 In a large bowl, combine the sliced apples, cranberries, and cooked bacon, then toss with the cheese sauce, chicken, and onions. Divide the apple mixture into four 6" ramekins. Place on a baking sheet and bake for 15 minutes until bubbly, then remove from oven. Cut the cooked bacon weave into 4 even 3" x 3" mini-weaves. Top each ramekin with a weave then bake for an additional 5 minutes.

Bacon Gorgonzola Green Bean Casserole

This recipe is guaranteed to impress your

Thanksgiving or Christmas dinner guests.

To prevent the sauce from burning, stir it

constantly during the entire process. Blanching

the green beans will give them a bright green

color and ensure that they are not overcooked.

WE RECOMMEND Baby Bubba's
Cinnamon Sugar Bacon

DRINK PAIRING *Rocco Recommends*
This dish will stand up well to a full-
bodied Cabernet Sauvignon or
Malbec from Robert Hall Winery in
Paso Robles, California.

MAKES 6 servings
PREP TIME 10 minutes
COOK TIME 40 minutes
TOTAL TIME 50 minutes

GREEN BEANS

- 4 cups water
- 1 teaspoon salt
- 4 cups fresh green beans, trimmed
- 2 cups bacon, chopped
- ½ cup yellow onions, diced
- 2 tablespoons flour
- 1 cup 2 percent milk
- ½ cup gorgonzola cheese
- 1 teaspoon garlic powder
- ½ teaspoon black pepper

TOPPING

- 1 cup pecans, chopped
- ½ cup uncooked bacon, chopped
- 2 tablespoons brown sugar
- ¼ teaspoon nutmeg

1 In a large pot, bring water and salt to a boil. Place ice and cold water in a large bowl. Cook the beans in the water for 10 minutes. Drain the beans then plunge them immediately into the ice-cold water. Set aside.

2 For the topping, preheat a large cast-iron skillet over medium-high heat. Toss the pecans, ½ cup chopped bacon, brown sugar, and nutmeg in a bowl and add to the skillet. Sugar will burn quickly, so stir often and scrape the pan to prevent burning. When the bacon is crispy, remove from pan and set aside.

3 Preheat oven to 350°F.

4 In the same pan, cook 2 cups chopped bacon over medium-high heat until crispy. Transfer bacon bits to a plate covered with paper towels, drain, and set aside. Heat the remaining bacon grease over medium heat and sauté onions until translucent.

5 Whisk in the flour, stirring constantly, and cook for 2 minutes. Slowly add in the milk and bring to a boil over medium-high heat. Cook until thick, about 1 minute. Reduce heat to low and add in cheese, a little at a time, until melted and the mixture is smooth. Add in the cooked bacon bits, garlic powder, and black pepper.

6 Toss the green beans and cheese sauce in a large casserole dish. Sprinkle the pecan topping on top and bake for 20–25 minutes. Serve immediately.

BACON FREAK

Burger Cheesebacon

In a bacon cheeseburger, the bacon plays second fiddle to the burger. It's high time for bacon to have the starring role in America's favorite meal. These patties are made with ground bacon and beef is used as the burger topping, in a role reversal that is long overdue. Serve with our Fully Loaded Bacon Beer Cheese Fries (see page 77) for the ultimate pigout!

WE RECOMMEND Boss Hog Hickory-Smoked Bacon

DRINK PAIRING Serve with your favorite beer. If you want something stronger, try a Tom Collins, the perfect summer cocktail.

MAKES 4 burgers

PREP TIME 10 minutes

COOK TIME 50 minutes

REST TIME 5–10 minutes

TOTAL TIME 65–70 minutes

½ pound bacon

1 medium onion, sliced into rings

½ pound lean ground beef
ground pepper

16 ounces steak
salt and pepper to taste

4 brioche buns

8 slices cheese

1 Cook the bacon in a 375°F oven until the fat starts to render out, but does not start to crisp, about 10 minutes. Remove from oven and chop finely. Reserve 2 tablespoons bacon grease.

2 Heat the bacon grease in a medium skillet over medium-high heat. Add onion and sauté for a few seconds, then turn the heat down to low and cook covered until caramelized, about 20 minutes, stirring occasionally. Set aside.

3 Combine the chopped bacon with ground beef and form into 4 uniform patties. Season each patty with pepper and cook on the BBQ until the internal temperature is at least 145°F, about 4–5 minutes per side. Bacon fat can easily catch fire, so cook over a low flame and keep a close eye on it.

4 Season the steak with salt and pepper, then cook until desired doneness, about 3 minutes on each side. Remove from the grill and rest for 5–10 minutes. Slice the steak into 1"-wide strips to resemble bacon strips.

5 When the patties are almost done, place each bun on the grill and top each patty with 2 slices of cheese. Allow the buns to toast and the cheese to melt. Turn off the heat and remove everything from the grill.

6 To make each burger cheesebacon, top the bottom bun with the cheese-covered patty, 4 ounces of steak, ¼ of the caramelized onions, and the top bun. Add your favorite burger toppings.

Bacon Shepherd's Pie

Shepherd's pie is proof that the British love meat and potatoes just as much as Americans do. With 2½ pounds of beef, pork, and bacon, simmered in a rich wine sauce and topped with the creamiest, dreamiest mashed potatoes, this dish represents comfort food at its finest.

WE RECOMMEND Jimmy's Garlic and Chive Bacon

DRINK PAIRING *Roberto Recommends* A hearty wine with good tannins to cut the fat, like a Syrah or old vine Garnacha or Grenache. A younger wine will accent the wine's fruitiness: an older wine will give a more funky flavor.

MAKES 10–12 servings

PREP TIME 15 minutes

COOK TIME 1 hour, 10 minutes

TOTAL TIME 1 hour, 25 minutes

MASHED POTATO TOPPING

- 4 large russet potatoes, peeled
- 5–6 cloves garlic, chopped
- 1 tablespoon salt
- 1 stick (½ cup) unsalted butter
- 1 cup half-and-half
- 1 teaspoon white pepper
- ½ cup bacon, cooked

FILLING

- 1 pound ground pork
- 1 pound ground beef
  salt and pepper
- ½ pound bacon, uncooked and coarsely chopped
- 1 large white onion, peeled and finely chopped
- 2 large carrots, peeled and chopped
- 3 cloves garlic, finely chopped
- 1 teaspoon fresh or dried rosemary, chopped
- 1 teaspoon fresh or dried thyme, chopped
- 2 tablespoons all-purpose flour
- 1 cup beef broth
- 1 cup dry, red wine
- 1 tablespoon tomato paste
- 1 cup English peas, fresh or frozen

1 Peel and cut the potatoes into small cubes. Place potatoes and garlic in a large pot, then cover with water. Salt the water and bring to a boil, and then simmer, partially covered, for 15–20 minutes or until tender.

2 While the potatoes are cooking, prepare the meat filling. Season the pork and beef with salt and pepper and brown the meat in a large Dutch oven or heavy pot until the meat is no longer pink. Transfer cooked meat to a bowl and set it aside. Drain the renderings from the pan and brown ½ pound of chopped bacon over medium heat until cooked, but not crispy. Using a slotted spoon, transfer the cooked bacon into a bowl with the ground beef, leaving 3 tablespoons of grease in the pot.

3 Cook the onion, carrots, garlic, rosemary, and thyme in the bacon drippings for 5 minutes, stirring occasionally. Add the meat mixture to the pot. Stir in the flour and cook for 1 minute. Add the broth, wine, and tomato paste, and bring to a boil. Reduce the heat to low, cover and simmer for 20–30 minutes until the sauce is thickened. Add the peas and remove from heat.

4 When the potatoes are cooked, drain well and return to the pot. Mash the potatoes, then add in the butter and half-and-half until creamy and smooth, adding a bit of extra half-and-half, if needed. Stir in the ½ cup chopped bacon and pepper until just combined. Add more salt and pepper to taste.

5 Spread the meat mixture into a large oven-safe dish. Top with the mashed potato mixture. Bake at 400°F until the potatoes are golden brown and crispy, about 20 minutes. For an extra-brown top, broil the pie for 5 minutes.

Bacon Chili Verde Pulled Pork

This pulled pork recipe is juicy and flavorful with a hint of spiciness. Let your slow cooker do all the work on a summer day when it's too hot to turn on the oven. Serve it on tortillas with your favorite taco fixin's, or on a bun with your favorite pulled pork sandwich toppings.

WE RECOMMEND Boss Hog Hickory-Smoked Slab Bacon

DRINK PAIRING This dish calls for a light, refreshing Mexican lager, like Corona or Dos Equis Lager.

MAKES 6–8 servings
PREP TIME 30 minutes
COOK TIME 6–8 hours
TOTAL TIME 6–8 hours, 30 minutes

PORK
- 6 fresh Anaheim peppers
- 5 cloves garlic, minced
  salt and pepper
- 1 pound slab bacon, cut into ½" cubes
- 1 yellow onion, chopped
- 2–3 tomatillos, chopped
- 1 pound pork shoulder
- 1 cup chicken broth

RUB
- 2 tablespoons dried oregano
- 4 teaspoons ground cumin
- 2 tablespoons olive oil
  salt and pepper

1 Roast peppers in a skillet over medium heat, rotating until skin is dark and flaky. Remove from heat and let cool. Carefully remove the skin and stems. Place roasted peppers, garlic, salt, and pepper in a bowl, and mash everything together.

2 Brown bacon in a large skillet over medium-high heat, about 10 minutes. Transfer to paper towels and reserve 2 tablespoons of the bacon grease. Cook the onions and tomatillos in the grease until the onions are transparent, about 3 minutes.

3 Combine the rub ingredients in a small bowl. Pat the pork shoulder dry then rub with the spices. Place pork shoulder, bacon cubes, chicken broth, mashed peppers, and tomatillo mixture in a slow cooker. Cook on low for 6–8 hours until the internal temperature of the pork is 165°F. When the meat is cooked, use 2 forks to pull the meat apart, then stir ingredients together.

Bacon
Beer Stew

Fall is our favorite season and this stew is the perfect autumn recipe.
Celebrate the cooler weather, the arrival of football season, and Oktoberfest
with this hearty, comforting stew. Serve it with warm, crusty,
buttered bread to soak up the delicious beer broth.

WE RECOMMEND Boss Hog Super-Thick Hickory-Smoked bacon

MAKES 6–8 servings

PREP TIME 15 minutes

COOK TIME 40 minutes

TOTAL TIME 55 minutes

- 1 pound slab or extra-thick-cut bacon, cubed
- 1 sweet onion, sliced into thin semicircles
- ½ head small green cabbage, cored, halved, and thinly sliced
- 2 celery stalks, sliced
- ½ teaspoon black pepper
- ½ teaspoon cumin
- ½ teaspoon salt
- 2 cloves garlic, finely diced
- 1 cup German-style lager beer
- 2 russet potatoes, peeled and cut into 1" cubes
- 2 carrots, peeled and sliced
- 2½ cups hot chicken stock
- 1½ tablespoons apple cider vinegar
- 1 tablespoon fresh parsley, chopped

1 Brown the cubed bacon in a large pot over medium-high heat for 5–7 minutes. Once the bacon starts to brown, add the onions and cook until golden brown and softened, 2–3 minutes. Add the cabbage and celery then cook until softened, about 2 minutes. Stir in the black pepper, cumin, and salt.

2 Stir in the garlic and cook until aromatic. Slowly stir in the cup of lager and cook for 3–4 minutes until slightly reduced. Stir in the potatoes, carrots, and chicken stock, then return to a boil. Once it begins to boil, cover partially and simmer on low for 40 minutes.

3 Finish the stew by stirring in the apple cider vinegar, chopped parsley, and additional salt, if needed. Serve with rye bread or rustic rolls.

Bourbon and Bacon
Sweet Potatoes

This sweet potato recipe is almost like a dessert! The candied bacon and pecan topping adds a sweet, crunchy texture to the creaminess of the boozy, buttery sweet potatoes. To make this dish more savory, you can eliminate the topping and sprinkle the top with crispy bacon bits before serving instead.

WE RECOMMEND Bourbon Street Vanilla Bourbon Bacon

DRINK PAIRING The classic Manhattan cocktail is the perfect accompaniment to this dish.

MAKES 12 servings

PREP TIME 15 minutes

COOK TIME 25–30 minutes

TOTAL TIME 40–45 minutes

SWEET POTATOES

- 4–5 cups sweet potatoes, peeled, diced
- ½ cup unsalted butter, melted
- ½ cup granulated sugar
- ⅓ cup bourbon
- 1 teaspoon vanilla extract
- 2 eggs, beaten
- 1 teaspoon kosher salt

TOPPING

- ¾ cup brown sugar
- ½ cup flour
- 6 tablespoons unsalted butter
- 1 cup chopped pecans
- 1 pound candied bacon (see page 16)

1 Preheat oven to 350°F and butter a 9" x 13" casserole dish.

2 Place the sweet potatoes in a large pot, and cover with water. Bring to a boil then reduce to a simmer. Cook over medium heat until tender. Drain and mash into a large bowl. Mix together the mashed sweet potatoes, melted butter, sugar, bourbon, vanilla, eggs, and salt. Spread the potato mixture in the casserole dish.

3 For the topping, mix the brown sugar and flour in a small bowl. Using a pastry cutter or a fork, cut in the butter until crumbly, then stir in the pecans. Sprinkle over the potatoes. Bake for 25–30 minutes until the top is brown and crisp. Cover the top with the chopped, candied bacon and serve.

Bacon Citrus Salad

This salad tastes like summer on a plate!

The made-from-scratch salad dressing is so

easy to prepare and so delicious that you'll never

go back to bottled dressing. This recipe will make

several servings of salad dressing and can be made

in advance. Feel free to experiment by adding

your favorite dried or fresh herb combinations.

WE RECOMMEND Pan-Fried Pier
Summer Herb Bacon

DRINK PAIRING A New Zealand
Sauvignon Blanc with its passion fruit
and tropical fruit overtones highlights
these bright, citrus flavors.

MAKES 1 salad

PREP TIME 10 minutes

COOK TIME 12 minutes

TOTAL TIME 25 minutes

DRESSING

- 1 small shallot, finely chopped
- ¼ cup white wine vinegar
- ¾ cup olive oil
- 3 tablespoons fresh orange juice
- 3 tablespoons fresh lemon juice
- 1 tablespoon bacon, cooked and
  finely chopped
- ½ teaspoon dried or fresh thyme
- ½ teaspoon dried or fresh rosemary

CHICKEN

- 1 chicken breast
  pepper to taste
- 2 strips bacon
- ¼ cup cooking wine

INGREDIENTS FOR THE SALAD

- 1 cup fresh baby spinach or spring
  mix
- ½ avocado, peeled and sliced
- ½ orange (naval or blood), peeled
  and separated into segments
- ½ grapefruit, peeled and separated
  into segments

1 To make the dressing, combine the chopped shallot
and vinegar in a small bowl. Allow to sit for 5 minutes.
Then pour all the dressing ingredients into a jar and shake
vigorously until well combined. Store the dressing in the refrigerator
until ready to use.

2 For the chicken, season the chicken breast with pepper, then
wrap it in bacon strips and secure with toothpicks, if needed. Heat
a small skillet over high heat. Sear the chicken breast for about
30 seconds on each side. Pour in the cooking wine and decrease
the heat to low. Cook covered for 8–10 minutes until the chicken's
internal temperature is 165°F. Remove from heat.

3 To assemble the salad, place the greens on a plate or in a large
bowl and arrange the avocado and citrus segments around the
edge of the dish. Slice the bacon-wrapped chicken breast and add
it to the salad. Drizzle with the bacon citrus dressing.

Bacon Basil Chicken Spiedini

LEVEL OF DIFFICULTY

This recipe is Steven Raichlen's. Steven is the author of the *Barbecue Bible* cookbook series and the host of *Project Smoke* and *Primal Grill* on public television. For more awesome barbecue recipes and helpful cooking tips, visit his website, Barbecuebible.com.

WE RECOMMEND Pan-Fried Pier Summer Herb Bacon

DRINK PAIRING Look for a cool-climate Sauvignon Blanc from the Loire Valley in France, or New Zealand. Its grassy, smoky, herbal notes complement the basil and the smoked cheese.

MAKES 12 skewers

PREP TIME 15–20 minutes

COOK TIME 15 minutes

TOTAL TIME 30–35 minutes

1½ pounds chicken tenders or boneless skinless chicken breasts
Coarse sea salt and freshly ground black pepper

12 ounces smoked mozzarella

12 wooden skewers, soaked in water

12 large fresh basil leaves

12 strips thin-sliced bacon butcher's string

1 12" x 18" piece of aluminum foil, folded into thirds, like a business letter

1 If you're using chicken tenders, remove the sinews. If you're using chicken breasts, cut them into 12 strips of roughly equal size and length. Season the chicken with salt and pepper. Slice the cheese into 12 finger-length strips. Skewer each chicken strip lengthwise, starting at one end and running lengthwise to the opposite end. Leave very little of the skewer's pointed tip exposed, as it will burn.

2 Lay a strip of cheese on each chicken skewer. Top with a basil leaf. Secure the basil leaf and cheese to the chicken by wrapping the piece of bacon around each chicken skewer. To keep the bacon from uncoiling as it cooks, tuck the top end of the bacon under the first winding and secure with butchers string.

3 Set up the grill for direct grilling and preheat to medium-high.

4 When you're ready to cook, brush and oil the grill grate. Place the folded aluminum foil grill shield toward the front of the grill grate. Arrange the spiedini on the grill grate, using the grill shield to protect the exposed ends of the skewers. Rotate the skewers every 2–3 minutes so the bacon browns evenly. If flare-ups occur, pull the spiedini forward so they're protected by the grill shield. When the fire dies down, return them to their original positions.

5 Transfer the cooked spiedini to a platter or plates. Serve immediately.

Chipotle Bacon Meat Loaf Sandwich

Chipotle peppers in adobo sauce have a tantalizing smoky flavor that greatly enhances the smokiness of bacon. This meat loaf recipe can easily be doubled and results in a juicy, meaty, fork-tender loaf.

LEVEL OF DIFFICULTY

WE RECOMMEND Lola's Chipotle Bacon

DRINK PAIRING *Roberto Recommends* Pair this with Aecht Schenkerla Rauchbier Marzen. Made with seriously smoked malt, this is meaty, intense, and satisfying. If you can't find it, try a smoked porter or black lager.

MAKES 4 sandwiches

PREP TIME 15 minutes

COOK TIME 30–35 minutes

REST TIME 5–10 minutes

TOTAL TIME 50–60 minutes

BACON MEAT LOAF

- 1 pound bacon, divided
- ½ cup whole oats
- ½ teaspoon cayenne
- ½ teaspoon chili powder
- ½ teaspoon dried thyme
- ½ onion
- 1–2 cloves garlic
- ¼ bell pepper
- ½ pound ground sirloin
- 1 teaspoon salt
- ¼ teaspoon black pepper
- 1 egg

CHIPOTLE SAUCE

- ¼ cup ketchup
- ¼ cup mayonnaise
- 1 teaspoon cumin
- 1 tablespoon Worcestershire sauce
- 2 chipotle peppers in adobo sauce, finely chopped
- 1 tablespoon adobo sauce
- 1 tablespoon honey

SANDWICH

- 4 slices pepper jack cheese
- 4 ciabatta rolls

1 Cook 1 pound of bacon until the fat starts to render out but it's not crispy. Continue cooking 8 strips of the bacon until crispy and set aside. Chop the lightly cooked bacon into bits.

2 Preheat oven to 350°F.

3 Prepare the chipotle sauce by whisking all ingredients together until smooth.

4 To make the meat loaf, combine in a food processor whole oats, black pepper, cayenne pepper, chili powder, and thyme. Pulse until it reaches a fine texture. Place in a bowl and set aside.

5 Combine onion, garlic, and bell pepper in the food processor. Pulse until fine, but not puréed.

6 Mix vegetables with chopped bacon and ground sirloin, then mix in the oatmeal mixture. Season with half of the chipotle sauce and salt, then add egg to combine. When the meat is well mixed, form into a loaf on a foil-lined baking sheet.

7 Bake the loaf at 350°F until the internal temperature reaches 155°F, about 30–35 minutes. Let it rest for 5–10 minutes before slicing into 4 even pieces.

8 Build a sandwich by adding cheese to a thick slice of meat loaf and top with a generous amount of chipotle sauce and 2 strips of bacon.

Creamy Bacon Lasagna

This reimagined lasagna is bursting

with big Italian flavors and savory bacon goodness.

The creamy, dreamy, white sauce is deliciously rich

and full of flavor contrasts, like sun-dried tomatoes,

mushrooms, and the crunch of crispy bacon.

Creamy Bacon Lasagna

WE RECOMMEND Rocco's Reserved
Sun-Dried Tomato Bacon
DRINK PAIRING *Rocco Recommends*
Carmenet Reserve Cabernet
Sauvignon is my favorite go-to red
wine for drinking with my favorite
Italian dishes. Medium-bodied,
fruity, and yet dry, it's a solid sipper.
MAKES 12 servings
PREP TIME 30 minutes
COOK TIME 30 minutes
TOTAL TIME 1 hour

CREAMY GARLIC SAUCE

- 8 cups (½ gallon) milk
- ½ cup butter
- 4 cloves garlic, minced
- ¾ cup flour
  pinch of salt
- ½ teaspoon black pepper
- ¼ teaspoon oregano
- ¼ cup grated parmesan cheese

LASAGNA

- 1 medium onion, diced
- 1 tablespoon olive oil
- ½ cup sun-dried tomatoes, chopped
- ½ cup fresh basil leaves, roughly chopped
- 1 cup crimini mushrooms, sliced
- 2 cups parmesan cheese, shredded
- 3 cups mozzarella cheese, shredded
- 10–12 lasagna noodles, cooked
- 1½ to 2 pounds chicken breast, cooked and diced
- 1 pound bacon, cooked rare and roughly chopped

1 Preheat the oven to 350°F. Lightly grease a
12" x 9" x 2½" baking dish. Cook lasagna noodles
according to package directions.

2 Heat milk in a large saucepan over medium heat; do not let it boil.

3 Melt butter in a large skillet, then sauté the garlic over medium
heat until soft and aromatic. Stir in flour and cook until thickened,
about 2 minutes.

4 Slowly add the hot milk to the flour mixture, whisking constantly
to avoid lumps. Simmer until thickened. Turn the heat off and whisk
in salt, black pepper, oregano, and parmesan cheese.

5 Sauté onions over medium heat in a small skillet with olive oil until
transparent about 7–10 minutes. Remove from heat, stir in sun-dried
tomatoes, basil, and mushrooms.

6 Combine the parmesan and mozzarella cheeses in a bowl.

7 Start assembling the lasagna by spreading a thin layer of the
sauce on the bottom of the baking dish. Layer 4 noodles over the
sauce, followed by another layer of sauce. Sprinkle ½ of the diced
chicken and ¼ of the bacon, followed
by ⅓ of the cheese mixture.

8 Next, sprinkle ½ of the vegetables and ¼ of the bacon. Repeat
noodles, sauce, chicken, bacon, cheese, veggies, and bacon again.
Add 1 more layer of 4 more lasagna noodles. Finish by topping the
noodles with the remaining sauce and cheese mixture.

9 Bake for 25–30 minutes, or until golden and bubbly.

Party Hardy

Bacon Bacon Truck Chili

LEVEL OF DIFFICULTY

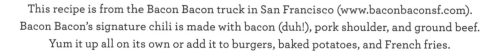

This recipe is from the Bacon Bacon truck in San Francisco (www.baconbaconsf.com). Bacon Bacon's signature chili is made with bacon (duh!), pork shoulder, and ground beef. Yum it up all on its own or add it to burgers, baked potatoes, and French fries.

WE RECOMMEND Boss Hog Hickory-Smoked Bacon

DRINK PAIRING Pair this meaty chili with a Flemish or Flanders red ale. If you can't find one, try the Red Trolley ale from Karl Strauss Brewing Company or the Irish red made by Samuel Adams.

MAKES 8 servings

PREP TIME 15 minutes

COOK TIME 1 hour, 45 minutes

TOTAL TIME 2 hours

- 1 pound of bacon, divided
- 2 cloves garlic
- 2 medium onions
- 1 red bell pepper
- ¼ cup chili powder
- 2 tablespoons paprika
- 1½ tablespoons ground cumin
- 1 tablespoon thyme
- salt and pepper to taste
- 2½ pounds ground beef
- ¼ pound pork shoulder, cooked and chopped
- 1½ cups pinto beans
- 4 ounces crushed tomatoes
- cheddar cheese, shredded
- cheddar crackers, for serving

1 In the large pot, cook the bacon over medium heat until lightly crisp, stirring occasionally. Remove ¼ of the bacon and set aside. Once the bacon is browned, add the garlic, onions, bell peppers, chili powder, paprika, cumin, and thyme, and season with salt and pepper to taste. When the onions are transparent, evenly spread out the mixture onto a parchment-lined tray to cool.

2 Add the beef and break it up with a wooden spoon, then add the chopped pulled pork. Stir in the beans and crushed tomatoes. Return the bacon mixture back to the pot, turn the heat down to low, and simmer for 1½ hours. Add additional salt and pepper to your liking, if needed. Chop up the reserved ¼ of cooked bacon into small bits. Serve the chili with a sprinkle of shredded cheddar cheese, bacon bits, and your favorite cheddar crackers.

Fully Loaded
Bacon Beer Cheese Fries

LEVEL OF
DIFFICULTY

You can't have loaded fries without an enormous amount of bacon,
and these highly shareable fries are no exception. Topped with
sour cream and green onions, these fries work well as a side to our
cheesebacon or sliders recipes. Or just have these for dinner instead!

WE RECOMMEND Beer Belly Beer-
Flavored Bacon

MAKES 2–4 servings

PREP TIME 10 minutes

COOK TIME 15–20 minutes

TOTAL TIME 25–30 minutes

  1   pound bacon, chopped
  2   tablespoons flour
  6   ounces beer, blonde or pale ale
1½   cups pepper jack, shredded
1½   cups mild cheddar cheese,
      shredded
  1   teaspoon black pepper
2–3 pounds french fries, cooked
      sour cream
      green onions, chopped

1 Cook the bacon in a large cast-iron skillet over medium-high heat until crispy, about 10–15 minutes. Transfer bacon to a plate lined with paper towels and set aside. Drain the bacon grease, reserving 2 tablespoons in the pan. Reduce heat to medium.

2 Whisk in the flour, cooking for 2 minutes. Slowly add in the beer and bring to a boil over medium-high heat, cook for 2–3 minutes. Reduce heat to low and gradually add in cheeses until melted and the mixture is smooth. Stir constantly to avoid burning. Stir in 2 cups bacon bits and the black pepper.

3 To serve, top the fries with warm cheese sauce, sour cream, the remaining bacon bits, and the green onions.

Bacon Blackberry
Goat Cheese Sliders

These sliders are extra moist and juicy, thanks to the addition of bacon in the patty. If you're not a goat cheese fan, you can substitute something else, but we recommend giving it a try. The tanginess of the goat cheese is complemented by the sweetness of the jam, the savory bacon, and the hint of black pepper spice. Grilling the sourdough adds a delicious crunchy texture.

WE RECOMMEND Baby Bubba's Butcher Block Hickory-Smoked Peppered Bacon

DRINK PAIRING *Roberto Recommends* In the summer, this is great with a dry rosé. Otherwise, something lighter and zippier like a Chianti or a lighter Zinfandel.

MAKES 10 sliders
PREP TIME 15 minutes
COOK TIME 30 minutes
TOTAL TIME 45 minutes

1	pound bacon, divided
½	pound lean ground beef
1	teaspoon garlic powder
1	teaspoon onion powder
1	sourdough baguette, cut into 20 thin slices
	butter or olive oil
5	ounces blackberry jam
10	ounces goat cheese, divided into 8 portions

1 Cook the bacon until the fat starts to render out, but does not start to crisp, about 8–10 minutes. Continue cooking 5 of the bacon strips until crispy and set aside.

2 Chop the lightly cooked bacon finely and combine with the ground beef, garlic powder and onion powder. Form into 10 even-shaped patties, roughly 3–4" in diameter. Grill each side for about 3–5 minutes until the internal temperature reaches 145°F.

3 While the patties are cooking, lightly coat each baguette slice with butter or oil and toast until golden, using a toaster or broiling on high for 2–4 minutes.

4 To assemble the sliders, place a beef and bacon patty on a slice of sourdough toast, topped with ½ strip of cooked bacon, 1 ounce of goat cheese, ½ tablespoon of jam, and another slice of sourdough toast. Serve immediately.

Bacon Apple Pie Nachos

These "nachos" are addictively delicious. The cinnamon sugar bacon brings out the sweetness in the apples and unites the smoky bacon and tart apple flavors. The flaky pie crust chips, the smooth bacon apple butter, and the crunchy topping combine to create an awesome flavor adventure in your mouth. Keep any extra bacon apple butter in the fridge and spread it on pancakes and waffles.

WE RECOMMEND Baby Bubba's Cinnamon Sugar Bacon or Orville's Apple Pie Bacon

DRINK PAIRING Try these nachos with a dry, hard cider, like Angry Orchard's Stone Dry Cider.

MAKES 4 servings

PREP TIME 15 minutes

COOK TIME 1 hour

TOTAL TIME 1 hour, 15 minutes

BACON TOPPING

- ¼ cup chopped bacon
- ¼ cup + 2 tablespoons all-purpose flour
- 3 tablespoons packed brown sugar
- 1 tablespoon granulated sugar
- 3 tablespoons cold unsalted butter, cut into small pieces

BACON APPLE BUTTER

- 1½ pounds Gala apples, peeled and diced
- ½ cup bacon, cooked and chopped
- ½ cup apple cider
- ¼ cup brown sugar
- ½ cup granulated sugar
- ½ teaspoon ground cinnamon
- ¼ teaspoon ground cloves

PIE CRUST "CHIPS"

- 3 cups all-purpose flour
- 2 tablespoons sugar
- 1½ sticks (¾ cup) cold unsalted butter, cut into small pieces
- 1 teaspoon ground cinnamon
- ¼ teaspoon ground cloves
- 1 teaspoon salt
- ⅓ cup cold vegetable shortening
- 8–10 tablespoons ice water

1 Preheat oven to 350°F.

2 To make the topping, combine the bacon, flour, and sugars in a medium bowl. Cut the butter into the dry mixture until pea-sized clumps form. Spread the mixture onto a parchment-lined jelly-roll pan and bake for 15–20 minutes until crispy. Remove from the pan and set aside to cool completely.

3 For the bacon apple butter, bring the apples, bacon, cider, and brown sugar to a rolling boil in a large pot over high heat. Leaving the lid slightly ajar, cover and boil until apples are tender, about 20 minutes. Stir every 5 minutes to prevent burning and promote even cooking.

4 Process cooked apples and cooking liquid in a blender or food processor until smooth, then return mixture back to the pan. Stir in granulated sugar, cinnamon, and cloves. Bring to a boil over high heat, then reduce to low and simmer uncovered until thickened, about 10 minutes. Cool for 20 minutes.

5 To make the chips, place the flour, sugar, cinnamon, cloves in a food processor and pulse to combine. Add the butter and shortening and pulse until the mixture forms pea-size pieces. Drizzle in 3 tablespoons of ice water and pulse again. Add more ice water if the dough seems too dry.

6 On a floured surface, roll out the dough to a ⅛" thickness and cut into 3" circles using a cookie or biscuit cutter. The dough makes about 60 "chips." Place on a parchment-lined baking sheet and bake for 8–10 minutes until the chips start to brown. Set aside to cool on a wire rack.

7 To assemble the nachos, layer the chips on a plate, drizzle the bacon apple butter on the chips, and sprinkle the bacon topping over the bacon apple butter.

Pretzel Bacon Grilled Cheese

with

Honey Mustard

We took a classic German-style pretzel

dough and turned it into a pretzel-shaped

grilled cheese sandwich that unites peppery

bacon, tangy mustard, and gooey cheese

into one awesome sandwich, fit for an

Oktoberfest snack feast or any time of year.

Pretzel Bacon Grilled Cheese with Honey Mustard

LEVEL OF DIFFICULTY

WE RECOMMEND Majestic Pig Cracked Four-Pepper Bacon

DRINK PAIRING Try a light witbier such as Blue Moon's Belgian white, Ommegang witte, or Einstök Icelandic white ale.

MAKES 6 sandwiches
PREP TIME 15 minutes
COOK TIME 30 minutes
REST TIME 1 hour, 15 minutes
TOTAL TIME 2 hours

PRETZEL DOUGH

- 1 packet instant or active dry yeast
- 1 tablespoon olive oil
- 1 cups warm milk
- ¾ cup warm water
- 1 teaspoon salt
- 3½ cups unbleached all-purpose flour, divided
- ½ cup bacon, cooked and chopped coarse Kosher salt for sprinkling

HONEY MUSTARD

- ¼ cup mayonnaise
- 2 tablespoons honey, warmed
- 2 tablespoons mustard
- 1 teaspoon horseradish (optional)

WATER BATH

- 6 cups water
- 1 teaspoon sugar
- 2 tablespoons baking soda

SANDWICH ASSEMBLY

- 12 thick slices sharp white cheddar or smoked cheddar cheese
- 12 bacon strips, cooked

1 In a large bowl, combine the yeast, oil, milk, and water. Add the salt and 2 cups of flour. Fold in the chopped bacon and gradually add in the remaining flour until a soft dough is formed. You may not need all the flour. Knead for 3–4 minutes and transfer to a greased bowl. Cover the dough with plastic wrap that has also been greased. Let the dough rise until it doubles in size, about 1 hour.

2 In a small bowl, whisk the mayonnaise, honey, mustard, and horseradish until smooth and then set aside.

3 When the dough has doubled in size, divide it into 6 even pieces. Using 1 section at a time, roll into a long strand and knot into a tight pretzel shape. Lay the pretzels on lightly greased parchment paper or a lightly floured countertop. Let rest, covered with a towel, for 15–20 minutes.

4 While the dough rests, preheat the oven to 425°F. Bring the water, sugar, and baking soda to a boil in a wide pot. When the water is hot, boil 1 pretzel at a time for 45–60 seconds on each side. With a slotted spoon, remove the dough from the boiling water, holding the pretzel in the slotted spoon for a few seconds so the extra water drips off. Place the boiled pretzels on parchment-lined baking sheets.

5 Bake for 15–17 minutes until a deep, golden brown. Let them cool for a few minutes and cut them in half to create a top and a bottom slice.

6 Preheat a buttered griddle or skillet to medium heat. Spread the mustard mixture on the cut side of 1 of the slices, and then layer 1 slice of cheese, 2 strips of bacon, and 1 more slice of cheese on top. Spread mustard on the cut side of the other slice and place it on top of the sandwich. Cook both sides on the griddle until they are crispy and the cheese is melted. Serve immediately.

BACON FREAK

BACON FREAK

Chipotle Bacon Street Tacos

These street tacos demand to be made for your next tailgate party or Super Bowl Sunday shenanigans. The chipotle rub imparts an addictive, smoky spiciness to the bacon and the creamy cilantro sauce cuts the spice.

WE RECOMMEND Boss Hog Hickory-Smoked Slab Bacon

DRINK PAIRING A minty mojito!

MAKES 20 tacos

PREP TIME 15 minutes

COOK TIME 15–20 minutes

TOTAL TIME 30–35 minutes

CHIPOTLE RUB

- 2 chipotle peppers in adobo sauce, finely chopped
- 4 teaspoons each ground cumin, garlic powder, onion powder, paprika, brown sugar

TACOS

- 2 pounds slab bacon
- 20 small corn tortillas, warmed
- 1 medium onion, chopped
- ½ bunch cilantro, chopped
- chipotle rub
- creamy cilantro sauce

CREAMY CILANTRO SAUCE

- ½ cup sour cream
- 1 chipotle pepper, chopped
- ½ bunch cilantro, chopped
- juice of 1 lime
- 1 clove garlic, chopped
- ½ teaspoon salt

1 Prepare the chipotle rub by mixing all ingredients together until well combined.

2 To make the cilantro sauce, combine all ingredients. The mixture should be just thin enough to pour.

3 Dice the slab into ¼" chunks and coat with the chipotle rub. Place in a large skillet and cook over medium-low heat for about 15–20 minutes until bacon chunks are cooked through and start to caramelize. Serve a heaping spoonful of chipotle bacon on each warmed corn tortilla, topped with a sprinkling of onions, cilantro, and a drizzle of creamy cilantro sauce.

Mango Mascarpone Bacon Quesadilla

Chutney is a food staple in many cultures, and for good reason. If you've never tried it, explore a new and exciting flavor combination with this recipe. With creamy mascarpone cheese and a punch of zingy, spicy chutney, this quesadilla strikes the perfect balance among sweet, tangy, and savory flavors.

WE RECOMMEND Boss Hog Hickory-Smoked Bacon

DRINK PAIRING Serve with Crabbie's Ginger Beer, an alcoholic ginger beer with a crisp, fizzy finish. Its zingy, ginger flavor stands up well to the spicy chutney.

MAKES 2 servings

PREP TIME 10 minutes

COOK TIME 30 minutes

TOTAL TIME 40 minutes

MANGO AND BACON CHUTNEY

- ¼ cup bacon, cooked and finely chopped
- 1 tablespoon diced onion
- 1 clove garlic, minced
- 1 cup fresh mango, diced
- ¼ cup golden raisins
- 2 tablespoons apple cider vinegar
- ¼ cup brown sugar
- ¼ teaspoon chili powder

QUESADILLA

- 4 ounces mascarpone cheese
- 2 12" tortillas
- 6 strips bacon, cooked and cut in half

1 In a medium saucepan, sauté the bacon until it starts to brown, then add the onion and garlic and cook until soft and fragrant. Stir in the mango, raisins, vinegar, brown sugar, and chili powder. Bring to a boil, and then lower heat to low and simmer, stirring frequently. Cook until thickened, about 20–30 minutes. Remove from heat.

2 Heat a buttered griddle over medium-high heat. Spread the mascarpone over one tortilla and top with cooked bacon strips. Spoon the chutney over the bacon and top with the other tortilla. Place on the griddle and cook both sides until the tortilla begins to brown, about a minute on each side. Cut the quesadilla into quarters and serve immediately.

Bacon-Wrapped BBQ Meatballs

You can't go wrong with a bacon-wrapped meatball, slathered in BBQ sauce. This recipe was created with carnivores in mind. Serve these meaty bites to your game day guests or bring them to a summer BBQ or potluck. They're a definite crowd pleaser!

WE RECOMMEND Boss Hog Hickory-Smoked Bacon

DRINK PAIRING Try Enegren Brewing Co.'s "Big Meat" Rauchbier with these little bites. The beechwood-smoked malt is balanced with Munich and caramel malts for a smoked, malty, caramel flavor that goes down smooth.

MAKES 32 meatballs

PREP TIME 20 minutes

COOK TIME 15–20 minutes

TOTAL TIME 35–40 minutes

- ½ pound ground beef
- ½ pound ground pork
- ½ cup bacon, chopped
- ⅓ cup breadcrumbs
- 1 egg, beaten
- 1–2 cloves garlic, minced
- ¼ cup sweet onion, very finely diced
- 1 teaspoon freshly ground black pepper
- 1 cup BBQ sauce
- 16 bacon strips cut in half
- 32 toothpicks, soaked in water

1 Preheat the oven to 400°F.

2 In a large bowl, mix together ground beef, ground pork, chopped bacon, breadcrumbs, egg, garlic, onion, and pepper. Mix the ingredients until just combined.

3 Scoop the meat mixture and form into 1" balls. Wrap ½ piece of bacon around each meatball until the ends overlap and secure with a toothpick. Place the meatballs on a parchment-lined baking sheet. Brush each meatball with BBQ sauce.

4 Bake for 15–20 minutes, until the bacon has browned and the internal temperature is 145°F.

Bacon-Wrapped Jam Pretzel Bombs

These pretzel bombs are an explosion

of sweet, salty, and savory flavors. The tangy,

sweet mustard bacon jam adds a plethora of

awesome flavors to your awestruck palate.

Keep any extra jam in the fridge and

add it to sandwiches or burgers for

a burst of tangy bacon flavor.

WE RECOMMEND Garlic Cracked-Pepper Bacon

DRINK PAIRING If these pretzel bombs are making you thirsty, pair them with your favorite German-style ale or lager.

MAKES 24 bombs

PREP TIME 5 minutes

COOK TIME 15–20 minutes

REST TIME 2 hours, 15 minutes

TOTAL TIME 2 hours, 40 minutes

LEVEL OF DIFFICULTY

DOUGH

- 1 packet instant (or active dry) yeast
- 1 tablespoon olive oil
- 1 cup warm 2 percent milk
- ¾ cup warm water
- 1 teaspoon salt
- 3½ cups unbleached all-purpose flour, divided

  Kosher salt for sprinkling

MUSTARD BACON JAM

- 1 pound bacon, chopped and uncooked
- 1 medium sweet onion, chopped
- 3 cloves garlic, chopped
- 1 teaspoon red chili flakes
- ¼ cup Dijon mustard
- ¼ cup vinegar
- ¼ cup maple syrup
- 2 tablespoons brown sugar
- 1 teaspoon smoked paprika

WATER BATH

- 3 quarts water
- 2 teaspoons sugar
- ¼ cup baking soda

ASSEMBLY

- 12 bacon strips, cooked and cut in half
- 24 toothpicks, soaked in water

1 To make the dough, combine the yeast, oil, milk, and water in a large bowl. Add the salt and 2 cups of flour. Gradually add in the remaining flour until a soft dough is formed; you may not need all the flour. Knead the dough for 3–4 minutes, then transfer the dough to a greased bowl. Cover the bowl with plastic wrap that has also been greased. Let it rise until it doubles in size, about 1–2 hours.

2 For the mustard bacon jam, cook bacon in a medium saucepan over medium heat until lightly browned and crispy. Transfer to a plate covered with paper towels. Pour out the bacon grease, keeping 2 tablespoons of grease in the saucepan. Add the onions, garlic, and chili flakes and cook over medium heat until the onions are translucent and tender, about 7–10 minutes.

3 Add the mustard, vinegar, maple syrup, brown sugar, and paprika. Bring to a boil, scraping up the brown bits on the sides and the bottom of the pan. Place the bacon back in the saucepan and simmer on low heat until the liquid is reduced and thick, about 30 minutes. Transfer to a food processor and pulse until chunks are small. Let it cool as you go on to the next step.

4 Working on a floured surface, divide the dough into 24 even pieces. Roll a piece of dough into a ball, then flatten it into a thin, flat disk. Place the dough in your hand, then spoon a teaspoon of bacon jam onto the disk. Gently close the dough over the jam, forming a little round ball. Pinch the open end together and twist to make a tight closure. Place the ball seam-side down to rest. Repeat with the remaining balls. Let each ball rest for 15 minutes.

5 Preheat the oven to 425°F. In a large saucepan, bring the water, sugar, and baking soda to a boil.

6 Gently spoon 3–4 balls into the boiling water, and boil for 45–60 seconds. With a slotted spoon, remove the balls from the boiling water. Place the boiled balls seam-side down on parchment-lined baking sheets, 1–2" apart.

7 Once the tray is filled, bake for 10 minutes until the balls start to brown. Remove from the oven and wrap each ball with ½ strip of bacon, securing with a toothpick. Return to the oven and bake until the balls are golden brown and the bacon is crispy, about 5 minutes.

Juicy Lucy
Bacon Fireballs

These fireballs have a spicy kick to them! Stuffed with pepper jack cheese and jalapeños, you can make them even spicier by substituting hotter chiles or peppers. Be careful cooking these on the barbecue, though, because bacon grease can easily catch fire.

WE RECOMMEND Coastal Caliente Jalapeño Bacon

DRINK PAIRING Tequila shots. 'Nuff said.

MAKES 12 fireballs

PREP TIME 15 minutes

COOK TIME 15–20 minutes

TOTAL TIME 30–35 minutes

- 2 pounds bacon, divided
- 1 pound ground beef
- 4 ounces pepper jack cheese, shredded
- 2 jalapeños, seeded and chopped
- 1 large onion
  wooden skewers, soaked in water
  BBQ sauce

1 Reserve 12 raw strips of bacon and cook the rest until the fat starts to render out, but does not start to crisp. Chop the cooked bacon finely, then combine with ground beef. Form into 12 uniform patties. Spoon some pepper jack cheese and jalapeños onto each patty, then form into a ball, sealing the cheese and jalapeños inside.

2 Cut off both ends of the onion and cut it in half. Using the smaller layers of onion, cup each fireball in 2 onion halves. Cut the larger layers into 4 pieces and use 2 of these pieces to cup a fireball. Wrap each fireball in 1 strip of uncooked bacon and secure with a wooden skewer.

3 Brush each of the fireballs with your favorite barbecue sauce, then grill them until the internal temperature reaches 145°F, about 15–20 minutes. Let them rest for 5 minutes, then serve warm.

The Ultimate Porker Bacon Weave Taco

This recipe is from Nick Chipman, creator and photographer of the food blog Dudefoods.com. Nick believes that, when it comes to food, bigger and crazier are usually better. Bacon is one of his favorite ingredients to experiment with. If you've seen a ridiculously awesome bacon weave creation on the Internet over the last few years, it probably came from Nick.

WE RECOMMEND Firecracker Chile Bacon

DRINK PAIRING Serve this beastly taco with a margarita rimmed with bacon salt.

MAKES 1 taco

PREP TIME 20 minutes

COOK TIME 6–8 hours

TOTAL TIME 6–8 hours, 20 minutes

PULLED PORK

2 tablespoons brown sugar

1 teaspoon salt

1 tablespoon ground cumin

1 tablespoon ground cinnamon

1 4–5 pound pork shoulder

1 large sweet onion, thinly sliced

1 cup chicken stock

BACON WEAVE SHELL

12 slices thin-cut bacon

1 regular taco shell

MAC & CHEESE

8 ounces elbow macaroni

1 cup bacon, chopped

2½ tablespoons all-purpose flour

2 cups milk

4 cups cheddar cheese, shredded

1 teaspoon pepper

1½ teaspoon salt

1 Combine the brown sugar, salt, cumin, and cinnamon in a small bowl. Rub the spice mixture evenly over the pork shoulder.

2 In the bowl of a slow cooker, place the onions in an even layer across the bottom, and pour in the chicken stock. Place the pork on top of the onions, cover and cook on high for 6–8 hours until tender, approximately 165°F.

3 Preheat the oven to 400°F an hour before the pork is ready.

4 For the bacon weave shell, make and cook a bacon weave (see page 18) using 12 slices of bacon.

5 Remove the bacon weave from the oven and blot off any excess grease with paper towels. Place a bowl upside down on the weave, and cut around the bowl with a knife to create a circular bacon weave.

6 Drape the circular bacon weave over a regular taco and bake again for 10 minutes or until the bacon shell is crispy and holds its shape. Remove the bacon weave taco shell from the regular taco shell and discard.

7 To make the mac & cheese, cook elbow macaroni according to package directions and set aside.

8 In a large saucepan, cook bacon over medium heat until it starts to brown. Whisk in the flour and cook for 2 minutes. Add milk slowly while stirring constantly. Reduce heat to low and slowly stir in cheese until it is completely melted. Add salt and pepper. Pour the cheese over the macaroni noodles and mix until the noodles are evenly coated.

9 Assemble the bacon weave taco by filling it half with pulled pork and half with mac & cheese. Serve immediately.

BACON FREAK

Bacon-Wrapped Chili Mango and Pineapple Spears

This appetizer is the perfect blend of sweet, savory, and spicy flavors. You can eliminate the chili powder if you don't like spicy foods. Have a napkin handy 'cause these are juicy and delicious!

WE RECOMMEND Soarin' Swine Applewood Smoked Bacon

DRINK PAIRING A fairly dry, mildly acidic Gewürztraminer perfectly complements the tropical fruity flavors.

MAKES 16 spears

PREP TIME 5 minutes

COOK TIME 15–20 minutes

TOTAL TIME 20–25 minutes

- 1   tablespoon chili powder
- ¼   cup brown sugar
-     zest of 1 lime, reserving the lime
- 2   mangos
- 1   pineapple
- 16 strips of bacon
- 16 toothpicks, soaked in water

1 Preheat barbecue to high heat.

2 Toss the chili powder, brown sugar, and lime zest in a bowl and set aside.

3 Peel and cut the mangos and cut each one into 8 uniform spears. Cut the pineapple into 16 uniform spears.

4 Cut the zested lime in half and rub it over the pineapple and mango spears. Place 1 pineapple spear and 1 mango slice together, then wrap them with 1 slice of bacon, securing with a toothpick. Repeat with the remaining fruit. Generously coat each bacon-wrapped spear with the sugar mixture.

5 Reduce heat to medium and sear the spears for about 30 seconds on each side. Lay a piece of foil on top of the grill and continue cooking the spears on the foil until the bacon is cooked through and crispy, about 15 minutes.

Bacon-Wrapped
Maple Brie Cheese

This recipe is from Amy Erickson, creator and photographer of the food blog Ohbiteit.com. Ohbiteit.com is known for its over-the-top, overly addictive recipes, many of which incorporate bacon. Creator Amy, who is not a trained chef and doesn't take food too seriously, likes to have fun and be creative in the kitchen. She chose the name for her website because it's what she says to anyone who dares to refuse to taste one of her recipes. It seems as if she's always chasing people with a fork and telling them to "open up!"

WE RECOMMEND Boss Hog Hickory-Smoked Bacon

DRINK PAIRING A lush Pinot gris from Oregon should have a good fruit/acid ratio to balance out the sweetness of the maple syrup and the pungent brie.

MAKES 4 servings

PREP TIME 5 minutes

COOK TIME 15–20 minutes

TOTAL TIME 20–25 minutes

1 pound thin-cut bacon
¼ cup good-quality maple syrup
1 8 oz wheel of brie cheese

1 Preheat oven to 350°F.

2 Create a bacon weave (see page 18) using all the bacon. Place the brie in the center of the bacon weave, and evenly brush the maple syrup onto all sides of the brie. Wrap the bacon weave around the brie and place it right side up on an oven-safe skillet.

3 Bake for 12–15 minutes until the bacon is golden and crispy. Broil for an additional 2–3 minutes until the bacon is super crispy.

4 Serve warm with crackers, chips, and any other "dippables" you'd like!

CHAPTER 6

Bacony Desserts

Deep-Fried, Bacon-Wrapped Brownie Bites

Sweet chocolate and savory bacon

are a one-two punch of complementary,

addictive flavors. If you're still not sold,

this recipe will convince you!

WE RECOMMEND Baby Bubba's
Cinnamon Sugar Bacon

DRINK PAIRING Serve these blissful
bites with a finger (or two) of brandy
or bourbon.

MAKES 36 bites

PREP TIME 15 minutes

COOK TIME 15–20 minutes

TOTAL TIME 30–35 minutes

BROWNIES

- ½ cup unsalted butter
- ½ cup granulated sugar
- ½ cup brown sugar, packed
- 1 teaspoon vanilla extract
- 2 eggs
- ½ cup flour
- ¼ heaping teaspoon baking powder
- ½ tablespoon espresso powder
- ¼ cup + 2 tablespoons cocoa powder
- ½ cup semisweet chocolate chips
- ½ cup bacon, cooked and finely chopped
- 18 bacon strips, cut in half

BATTER

- 3 eggs
- ¼ cup sugar
- 2 cups milk
- 3⅔ cups flour
- ½ teaspoon salt
- 2 teaspoons baking powder
- 1 teaspoon vanilla extract
  vegetable oil, for frying
  powdered sugar, for dusting
  the bites

1 Preheat oven to 325°F.

2 In a large bowl, cream butter and sugars. And vanilla and eggs and mix until smooth. Mix dry ingredients together in a medium bowl. Gradually add dry ingredients into the wet ingredients. Fold chocolate chips and bacon bits into the batter.

3 Spoon 1 tablespoon brownie batter in each cup of a greased mini–muffin tin. Fill each cup ⅔ full with brownie batter. Bake for 15 minutes until an inserted toothpick comes out clean. Remove from oven and cool.

4 Wrap ½ strip of cooked bacon on top of each brownie bite and secure with a toothpick.

5 Preheat a deep fryer or heat 1" of oil in a deep pan to 350°F.

6 Prepare the batter by beating eggs and sugar together in a large mixing bowl. Slowly whisk in the milk and vanilla extract until well incorporated. Add dry ingredients and whisk until smooth.

7 Spoon the batter over the bites and fry them 2 at a time in hot oil until the batter is golden brown, about 1–2 minutes on each side. Transfer to a plate lined with paper towels to drain. Serve warm with a dusting of powdered sugar.

Maple Bacon Macarons

Macarons might look hard to make, but they're easy once you get the hang of it. The trick is not to overmix the batter and to pipe it evenly so the macarons are uniform in size. These macarons are full of sweet maple flavor and a hint of smoky bacon. They're an impressive gift for your favorite bacon fan.

Maple Bacon Macarons

LEVEL OF DIFFICULTY

WE RECOMMEND Boss Hog Hickory-Smoked Maple Bacon
DRINK PAIRING A flute of dry champagne complements the elegance of these dainty macarons, bursting with big flavor.
MAKES 25–30 macarons
PREP TIME 15 minutes
COOK TIME 13–15 minutes
REST TIME 15 minutes–1 hour
TOTAL TIME 43 minutes–1½ hours

SHELL

- 1 cup powdered sugar
- ¾ cup almond flour
- 2 egg whites, room temperature red and copper food coloring (optional)
- 1 teaspoon maple extract (do not use maple syrup)
- ¼ cup granulated sugar
- 2 strips bacon, cooked and finely chopped

FILLING

- ¾ cup powdered sugar
- ¼ cup butter, softened
- ½ teaspoon maple extract brown gel food coloring (optional)
- 5–6 slices bacon, cooked crispy, cut into 25–30 pieces, one for each cookie

1 Line 2 cookie sheets with parchment paper.

2 Place powdered sugar and almond flour in a food processor and pulse into a fine powder for about 1 minute. Sift into a medium bowl, discarding large pieces.

3 In the large bowl of an electric mixer, beat the egg whites at medium speed until foamy using the whisk attachment. Dip the end of a toothpick into the food coloring and add a drop of each color to the egg whites. Add maple extract and beat using the whisk attachment a few seconds longer. With the mixer on full speed, slowly add the granulated sugar and beat using the whisk attachment for 2–3 minutes until stiff, shiny peaks form. Scrape down the sides of the bowl.

4 Sift half of the almond flour mixture into the whipped whites, then toss in the chopped bacon. Fold in gently until just combined. Fold in the remaining flour mixture until just combined. Be careful not to overmix, as this will flatten the eggs. The batter should be smooth and shiny with peaks that quickly relax when dropped on a plate.

5 Preheat oven to 350°F. Using a ½" piping tip, pipe batter into 1½" circles about 2" apart on the lined baking sheets. Gently tap the cookie sheets on the counter to remove any air bubbles. Allow the macarons to rest for 15–60 minutes until the tops are stiff but do not stick when touched with your finger.

6 Bake 1 sheet at a time for 13–15 minutes, rotating halfway through. Remove from oven and allow cookies to cool completely.

7 For the filling, beat the powdered sugar and butter in a bowl until light and fluffy, about 2 minutes. Add maple extract and food coloring, then beat until smooth.

8 When the cookies have cooled, match similar-sized shells and pipe or spread a small amount of frosting on each shell. Sandwich a small piece of bacon between the two frosted shells and repeat with remaining shells. Serve immediately or store in the refrigerator in an airtight container. Remove from the refrigerator 30 minutes before serving.

BACON FREAK

Angry Orchard
Crisp Bacon Truffles

This recipe is from Angry Orchard Hard Cider. Today's home cooks and chefs are increasingly interested in experimenting with hard cider in their culinary creations. Bacon and cider paired together achieve the classic sweet and savory flavor profile and that delectable combo really shines in these truffles. With only 5 ingredients, they're also incredibly easy to make.

~~~~~~~

WE RECOMMEND Boss Hog
Hickory-Smoked Bacon

MAKES 24 truffles

PREP TIME 10 minutes

COOK TIME 15 minutes

REST TIME 30 minutes

TOTAL TIME 55 minutes

½ pound smoked bacon, sliced thin

1 cup Angry Orchard Crisp Cider,
divided

½ cup brown sugar

8 ounces baking chocolate

1 cup cocoa powder

1 Place bacon in a skillet, pour ½ cup cider over the bacon, and sprinkle brown sugar. Cook over medium heat until reduced, and bacon is cooked and slightly crispy. Remove from the pan and chop the bacon.

2 In a microwave-safe container, microwave baking chocolate and remaining cider on defrost (low), for 6 minutes, or until soft. Remove, and whisk until smooth. Whisk in bacon mixture, and let cool.

3 Roll into truffles with your hands or a scoop, and roll in the cocoa powder. Chill until set, about half an hour.

Bourbon Bacon Pecan Bars

We put all the deliciousness of bourbon bacon

pecan pie into these dessert bars. These

bacontastic beauties are real crowd pleasers.

WE RECOMMEND Bourbon Street
Vanilla Bourbon Bacon
DRINK PAIRING Whether you like
it neat, straight up, or on the rocks,
imbibe your favorite brand of
bourbon with this delectable dessert.
MAKES 12 bars
PREP TIME 10 minutes
COOK TIME 30 minutes
TOTAL TIME 40 minutes

CRUST

1½ sticks (¾ cup) unsalted butter
¼ cup sugar
1 large egg yolk
1½ cups all-purpose flour

FILLING

3 eggs
¾ cup brown sugar, packed
⅔ cup corn syrup
1 teaspoon vanilla extract
2 tablespoons melted butter
2 tablespoons bourbon
1½ cups toasted pecans, roughly
chopped
1 pound bacon, cooked chewy,
divided
¾ cup semisweet or bittersweet
chocolate chips

1 Preheat oven to 350°F. Line a 9" x 13" casserole dish with parchment paper and lightly grease it, including the sides. Let the paper hang just over the sides for easy removal later.

2 In a medium bowl, beat the butter, sugar, and egg yolk at medium speed until blended. Add the flour and mix until crumbs form. Do not overmix. Press the dough evenly into the bottom of the casserole dish.

3 For the filling, whisk together in a large bowl the eggs, brown sugar, corn syrup, vanilla, melted butter, and bourbon. Stir in the pecans, 1 cup chopped bacon, and the chocolate. Pour pecan mixture over the crust.

4 Bake for 25–30 minutes. Remove from the oven and top with the remaining slices of bacon. Return to the oven for another 5–10 minutes until the filling expands but is still slightly wiggly. Let it cool completely. Run a knife along the edges of the pan, then carefully remove the parchment paper to release the bars. Cut into squares and serve.

Please, Sir, I Want S'mores!

The delicousness of s'mores shouldn't be confined to the campfire. We took everything you love about this beloved camping treat and made it into this impressive cake that lets you enjoy the taste of s'mores without all the hassles of camping.

Please, Sir, I Want S'mores!

WE RECOMMEND Boss Hog Hickory-Smoked Maple Bacon

MAKES 12 servings

PREP TIME 25 minutes

COOK TIME 45–60 minutes

TOTAL TIME 1 hour, 10 minutes–1 hour, 25 minutes

GRAHAM CRACKER CRUST

10–12 graham crackers

¼ cup flour

2 tablespoons brown sugar

1 egg, beaten

⅓ cup butter, melted

CHOCOLATE CAKE

3 ounces dark chocolate, chopped

¾ cup coffee, brewed

2 large eggs

1½ cups sugar

¼ cup canola oil

2 tablespoons bacon grease

1 teaspoon vanilla extract

1¼ cups all-purpose flour

½ cup dark cocoa powder

1 teaspoon baking soda

½ teaspoon baking powder

½ teaspoon salt

¾ cup buttermilk

1 cup bacon, cooked and finely chopped

MARSHMALLOW FILLING

4 cups marshmallows

¾ cup milk

2 cups whipping cream, whipped

½ cup bacon, cooked and chopped

ASSEMBLY

1 pound bacon, cooked and finely chopped

1 Preheat oven to 325°F.

2 To make the crust, place the graham crackers, flour, and brown sugar into a food processor and pulse into a fine powder. Add the egg and butter and form into a crust. Press into the bottom of a parchment-lined 9" round cake pan. Bake for 15–20 minutes until the crust starts to brown and remove from the oven. Leave the oven on.

3 For the chocolate cake, grease two 9" baking pans and line the bottoms with parchment paper. Set aside.

4 Combine chocolate and coffee in a small bowl. Whisk until smooth. In a large bowl, beat the eggs. Gradually mix in the sugar, oil, grease, vanilla, and the chocolate mixture until well combined. In a separate bowl, mix the flour, cocoa powder, baking soda, baking powder, and salt. Add half the dry ingredients to the wet ingredients, and then stir in half the buttermilk, mixing well between additions. Repeat with the remaining half of the dry mixture and buttermilk. Fold in the bacon.

5 Pour the batter evenly into the prepared pans. Bake for 30–40 minutes until a toothpick inserted in the center comes out clean. Remove from the oven and cool for 5 minutes, then remove cake from the pans and cool them on a wire rack.

6 For the marshmallow filling, combine the marshmallows and milk in a large saucepan. Heat over low heat until the marshmallows are melted, stirring constantly. Remove from heat and let cool. Fold in the whipped whipping cream and bacon bits and cool in the refrigerator.

7 To assemble the cake, place the graham cracker crust on the center of a cake plate. Spread ⅓ of the marshmallow filling on top of the crust. Place a chocolate cake on top of the filling. Spread another ⅓ of the filling on top of the cake. Sprinkle half the bacon on the filling, followed by the other cake. Top with the remaining filling and the remaining bacon. Decorate with whipped cream, marshmallows, and drizzle with chocolate if desired.

BACON FREAK

BACON FREAK

Bacon Chocolate Challah Bread Pudding

This recipe is for our Jewish fans who still partake of bacon every now and then. Challah's thick, chewy texture is the ideal vehicle for bread pudding since it doesn't get soggy. This recipe is incredibly easy to make and incredibly delicious to eat. Let the dairy come to room temperature so the butter won't solidify when it's added.

WE RECOMMEND Bourbon Street Vanilla Bourbon Bacon

DRINK PAIRING A smooth nitro stout or milk stout complements the chocolate flavors and richness of the bread pudding.

MAKES 12 servings

PREP TIME 20 minutes

COOK TIME 1 hour

COOLING TIME 15 minutes

TOTAL TIME 1 hour, 35 minutes

- 1 loaf challah
- 4 eggs
- 2 cups 2 percent milk
- 2 cups half-and-half
- 1 cup granulated sugar
- 1 tablespoon vanilla extract
- ½ teaspoon salt
- ½ cup unsalted butter, melted
- 10 ounces dark chocolate chips
- 1 pound candied bacon (see page 16)

1 Heat oven to 250°F. Cut or tear the challah into 1–1½" chunks. Place pieces of challah in a single layer on baking sheets and toast in the oven for 5–7 minutes until slightly toasted. Remove from oven and let cool.

2 In a large bowl, beat the eggs then add the milk, half-and-half, sugar, vanilla extract, salt, and butter, and mix. Add the toasted bread to the liquid and mix until all the bread is wet. Add the chocolate and half the candied bacon until combined. Butter a 9" x 13" casserole or baking dish and then add the bread mixture.

3 Bake for 1 hour or until a toothpick inserted in the middle comes out clean. Cool for 15 minutes before cutting. Top each piece with a dollop of whipped cream and drizzle with chocolate syrup if desired. Sprinkle remaining bacon on top and serve warm.

Bacon Peanut Butter Cup Melt

These peanut butter cup melts are an ooey, gooey mess! Peanut butter, chocolate, honey, and bacon combine to create an addictive flavor combo. Substitute King's Hawaiian® sweet rolls if you don't have time to make sweet rolls from scratch. Grab a napkin and dig in.

WE RECOMMEND Sweet Cheeks
Honey-Glazed Bacon

DRINK PAIRING Go completely over
the top by pairing this with a peanut
butter beer like Belching Beaver's®
peanut butter milk stout, Blue
Moon Brewing Company's® peanut
butter ale, or Karl Strauss Brewing
Company's® peanut butter cup porter.

MAKES 1 melt

PREP TIME 15 minutes

COOK TIME 30 minutes

REST TIME 1½ hours

TOTAL TIME 2 hours, 15 minutes

SWEET BACON ROLLS

- 1   package yeast
- 2   cups warm milk
- 3   tablespoons butter, melted
- ½   cup sugar
- 4½ cups all-purpose flour, divided
- ½   cup bacon, lightly cooked and
      chopped

EACH MELT

- 1   sweet bacon roll
      honey
- 2   peanut butter cups
- 1   strip of bacon, cooked

1 To make the rolls, dissolve the yeast in warm milk (110°–115°F) in a
large bowl. Add the butter, sugar, 3 cups flour, and chopped bacon,
beating until smooth. Add an additional 1–1½ cups of flour to form
a soft dough.

2 Knead the dough for 5–7 minutes on a floured surface until
smooth and elastic. Place the dough in a greased bowl. Cover with
a piece of greased plastic wrap and allow to rise until doubled in
size, about 1 hour.

3 Knead the dough a few times to deflate it and then divide it into
16 pieces. Shape each piece into a ball and place them 2" apart
on parchment-lined baking sheets. Cover and allow to rise until
doubled in size, about 30 minutes. Heat oven to 350°F and bake the
rolls for 25 minutes until golden brown. Brush the tops with warm
honey and let the rolls cool.

4 To make the melt, cut a roll in half and spread honey on both
sides. Cut the peanut butter cups in half, then assemble onto the
roll so they fit nicely. Top with 2 half-strips of bacon. Cook on a
350°F panini press or a buttered griddle for 3–5 minutes until cups
are melted and bread is crispy. Drizzle with more honey and serve
warm.

Three-Cheese Bacon Peach Cobbler

Made with sweet, ripe peaches, a blend of three savory cheeses, and lots of crispy, salty bacon, you'll devour this cobbler by the plateful. Be sure to use fresh peaches. To pick the perfect peach, choose those that just give slightly when the flesh is gently squeezed. If they're too firm or too squishy, chances are they're too ripe or not ripe enough.

Three-Cheese Bacon Peach Cobbler

LEVEL OF
DIFFICULTY

WE RECOMMEND Sweet Cheeks honey-glazed bacon

DRINK PAIRING Serve this with a Bellini, a mix of Prosecco sparkling wine and peach purée or nectar.

MAKES 12 servings

PREP TIME 25 minutes

COOK TIME 45 minutes

TOTAL TIME 70 minutes

CHEESE BLEND

- 4 ounces ricotta cheese
- 8 ounces cream cheese, softened and diced
- 2 ounces asiago cheese, shredded

FILLING

- 6 medium peaches, sliced
- 1 cup bacon, cooked and roughly chopped, divided
- 2 tablespoons honey
- ½ cup granulated sugar
- 1 teaspoon cinnamon
- ½ teaspoon ginger
- ½ teaspoon nutmeg

BATTER

- 1 cup flour
- 1 cup sugar
- 2 teaspoons baking powder
- 1 egg, at room temperature
- ⅔ cup milk, at room temperature
- ½ cup melted butter
- 1 cup bacon, cooked and roughly chopped, divided

1 Preheat oven to 350°F.

2 For the cheese blend, mix together ricotta, cream cheese, and asiago cheese in a medium bowl until well combined. Set aside.

3 For the filling, mix together sliced peaches and 1 cup bacon in a large bowl. Toss with the honey. In a small bowl, stir together granulated sugar, cinnamon, ginger, and nutmeg. Toss the sugar mixture with the peaches and set aside.

4 For the batter, mix together flour, sugar, and baking powder. Beat the egg and milk together and then pour into the flour mixture. Whisk until smooth.

5 Pour melted butter in a 9" x 13" baking dish, then pour the batter evenly over the melted butter. Drop spoonfuls of the cheese mixture over the batter, but do not mix together. Sprinkle 1 cup of chopped bacon over the cheese, and then pour the peaches on top.

6 Bake for 40–45 minutes until the batter rises up to the edge and is golden brown. Let it rest for a few moments, then serve warm.

BACON FREAK

Peanut Butter
Candied Bacon Ice Cream

This recipe is from Coolhaus. Cofounders Natasha Case and Freya Estreller started baking cookies, making ice cream, and combining them into mobile "cool houses" in 2008. Now, Coolhaus operates a national fleet of twelve mobile ice cream trucks and carts (five in southern California, two in New York City, and five in Dallas). For architecturally inspired gourmet ice cream, visit Eatcoolhaus.com.

WE RECOMMEND Boss Hog Hickory-Smoked Bacon

DRINK PAIRING Make an affogato: Mix a shot of espresso with a scoop (or three) of this peanut butter candied bacon ice cream. Add a shot of coffee liqueur and you've got the ultimate adults-only sundae.

MAKES 1½ quarts
PREP TIME 15 minutes
COOK TIME 15 minutes
REST TIME 14–26 hours
TOTAL TIME 14–26 hours, 30 minutes

CUSTARD BASE
- 3 cups whole milk
- 1 cup heavy cream
- 1½ cups granulated sugar, divided
- 8 large egg yolks

1 Start by making the custard base. Use the freshest eggs possible for the best results. If possible, chill the base for a full 24 hours—the longer, the better. We like to refrigerate our bases in plastic or stainless-steel pitchers with airtight lids for easy pouring into the ice cream maker after chilling.

2 In a 4-quart saucepan, combine milk, cream, and half the sugar. Set over high heat, and cook, stirring occasionally, until mixture comes to a boil, about 5 minutes.

3 Meanwhile, in a medium bowl, whisk yolks and remaining sugar until smooth, heavy, and pale yellow, about 30 seconds.

4 When the cream mixture just comes to a boil, whisk, remove from heat, and, in a slow stream, pour half the cream mixture over the yolk-sugar mixture, whisking constantly until blended.

5 Return pan to the stovetop over low heat. Whisking constantly, stream yolk-cream mixture back into the pan.

6 With a wooden spoon, continue stirring until the mixture registers 165°F–180°F on an instant-read thermometer, about 2 minutes. Do not heat above 180°F or the eggs in the base will scramble. Mixture should be slightly thickened and coat the back of the spoon, with steam rising, but not boiling. (If you blow on the back of the spoon and the mixture ripples, you've got the right consistency.)

ICE CREAM FLAVORINGS

- 4 tablespoons (½ stick) butter
- 8 1-ounce strips bacon
- ½ cup maple syrup
- ½ teaspoon sea salt
- 4 ounces natural peanut butter, at room temperature
- 1 teaspoon kosher salt

7 Pour the base into a clean container and refrigerate for 12 to 24 hours. Use the base within 3 to 5 days.

8 For the ice cream flavorings, melt the butter in a small saucepan over medium heat. Cook until it is a medium brown/caramel color, being careful not to burn it, about 4 minutes. Strain the melted butter through a fine-mesh sieve into a small bowl. Set aside to cool.

9 In a large skillet, cook the bacon strips over medium-low heat, turning, until just before crispy. Transfer the cooked bacon to a paper towel–lined plate to drain and cool.

10 Finely dice the cooled bacon. In a clean skillet, combine diced bacon and syrup and cook over medium-high heat for about 3 minutes, until syrup is thick and has reduced by half. Sprinkle with sea salt. Set candied bacon aside to cool.

11 Mix peanut butter and kosher salt into the base with an immersion blender or a hand mixer. Stir the cooled brown butter and candied bacon into the custard base. Mix well to combine. Process the mixture in an ice cream maker according to the manufacturer's instructions. Scrape into an airtight storage container. Freeze for a minimum of 2 hours before serving.

Maple Bacon Gingerbread Roulade

Looking for a dessert recipe that will seriously impress your Christmas dinner guests with both its presentation and its flavor? Look no further! This roulade is as delicious as it is elegant. The smoky bacon perfectly complements the fragrant gingerbread cake and sweet maple filling. The trick to rolling the roulade is not to overbake the cake; a dry, crumbly cake is more likely to crack.

Maple Bacon Gingerbread Roulade

WE RECOMMEND Rita Hogsworth
Maplewood Smoked Bacon
DRINK PAIRING A brandy Alexander
garnished with nutmeg.
MAKES 8–10 servings
PREP TIME 25 minutes
COOK TIME 15 minutes
REST TIME 2 hours, 30 minutes
TOTAL TIME 3 hours, 10 minutes

BACON GINGERBREAD

- 6 large eggs, separated
- ½ cup + 2 tablespoons granulated sugar
- ¼ cup brown sugar
- 2 tablespoons unsalted butter, melted
- 1 tablespoon light molasses
- 1 teaspoon vanilla extract
- ¾ cup all-purpose flour
- 1 teaspoon baking powder
- 1½ teaspoons ground ginger
- 1½ teaspoons ground allspice
- ¼ teaspoon salt
- ½ cup bacon, cooked
- 1 teaspoon cream of tartar
  Powdered sugar

MAPLE FILLING

- ¾ cup whipping cream, chilled
- ¼ cup sour cream, chilled
- ¼ cup powdered sugar
- 2 tablespoons brown sugar
- 2 tablespoons maple syrup, plus some for topping
- 8 strips bacon, cooked

SUGAR TOPPING

- 2 tablespoons powdered sugar
- 1 tablespoon brown sugar

1 For the bacon gingerbread, preheat oven to 350°F. Line a 15½" x 10½" x 1" baking sheet with waxed paper that has been buttered and floured.

2 In the bowl of a stand mixer, beat the egg yolks, ½ cup of granulated sugar, and the brown sugar for about 5 minutes. Beat in the melted butter, light molasses, and vanilla extract. In a separate bowl, combine the flour, baking powder, ginger, allspice, and salt. Sift this dry mixture over the egg mixture and fold in gently. Fold in the chopped bacon.

3 In another separate bowl, beat the egg whites and the cream of tartar until soft peaks form. Add the remaining 2 tablespoons of granulated sugar, beating until stiff. Carefully fold the whites into the egg mixture in 3 batches. Pour the batter into the prepared baking sheet, using a spatula to even out the surface.

4 Bake for 15 minutes or until a toothpick inserted in the middle comes out clean. Carefully cut around the sides of the pan to loosen the cake. Place a clean, dry kitchen towel on the countertop and dust the towel with powdered sugar. Place the pan upside down on the towel, discarding the waxed paper. Gently roll the warm cake with the towel, beginning at the long side of the cake. Roll the cake carefully so it doesn't crack. Allow the rolled-up cake to cool for at least 30 minutes.

5 For the maple filling, beat the whipping cream, sour cream, powdered sugar, brown sugar, and maple syrup in a medium bowl until combined. Unroll the cake and remove the towel. Spread the filling over the entire surface of the cake then place 8 strips of cooked bacon on the filling, parallel with the short edges of the cake. Carefully, roll up the cake so it is tight, but does not break apart. Place seam-side down on a rectangular dish and refrigerate until set, at least 2 hours.

6 Whisk together the powdered sugar and the brown sugar. Sprinkle on the cake, slice, and serve with a drizzle of maple syrup and a dusting of powdered sugar.

After-Dinner Doughnut Holes

LEVEL OF DIFFICULTY

Coffee and doughnuts go together like bacon and chocolate, so we combined all four into a delicious after-dinner treat.

WE RECOMMEND Bourbon Street Vanilla Bourbon Bacon

MAKES 36 doughnut holes

PREP TIME 15 minutes

COOK TIME 15–20 minutes

REST TIME 3 hours

TOTAL TIME 3 hours, 35 minutes

INGREDIENTS

¾ cup all-purpose flour

½ cup unsweetened cocoa powder

2 tablespoons espresso powder

1 teaspoon baking powder

2 large eggs

¾ cup sugar

2 tablespoons buttermilk

2 tablespoons coffee-flavored liqueur

1½ tablespoons butter, melted

½–1 cup bacon, cooked and finely chopped

vegetable oil

powdered sugar

1 In a large mixing bowl, combine the flour, cocoa powder, espresso powder and baking powder. In a medium bowl, whisk the eggs, sugar, buttermilk, and liqueur. Stir the wet ingredients into the dry ingredients then add in the melted butter, stirring until blended. Fold in the bacon, cover the dough, and chill for 3 hours.

2 Scoop the dough out onto a well-floured surfaced and roll the dough into 1" balls with floured hands. Set the balls on a floured baking sheet.

3 Fill a large pan with 2" of oil and heat to 375°F. One at a time, drop 5–6 doughnuts into the oil. Cook for 2 minutes on each side, then transfer the doughnuts to a paper towel to drain.

4 When the doughnuts are cooled, roll them in powdered sugar until nicely coated.

Bacon Mocha Martini

When alcohol joins the bacon + chocolate party, it's a match made in hog heaven. With coffee liqueur and a candied bacon strip, this martini is the breakfast of champions.

WE RECOMMEND Rita Hogsworth Maplewood Smoked Bacon
MAKES 1 martini
TOTAL TIME 2 minutes

INGREDIENTS

- 1 ounce bacon-flavored vodka
- 1 ounce chocolate liqueur
- 1 ounce coffee liqueur
- 1 ounce half-and-half or heavy cream
- 1 candied bacon strip (see page 16)
  chocolate syrup (optional)

1 Combine all ingredients over ice in a cocktail shaker and shake until the outside of the shaker is frosted. If desired, squeeze a little chocolate syrup in the bottom of a martini glass and then pour the drink into the glass. Garnish with a strip of candied bacon.

Salted Caramel Bacon Pie Bites

These mini-pies ooze salted caramel

flavor. The homemade caramel sauce

makes them addictively delicious.

WE RECOMMEND Baby Bubba's Apple Cinnamon Bacon

DRINK PAIRING Warm your tummy and bring out the rich, caramel flavors by serving these sweet little pies with hot buttered rum

MAKES 24 pie bites

PREP TIME 20 minutes

COOK TIME 10 minutes

REST TIME 30 minutes

TOTAL TIME 1 hour

PIE CRUST

- 3 cups all-purpose flour
- 1 teaspoon salt
- 2 tablespoons sugar
- 1½ sticks cold unsalted butter, cut into small pieces
- ⅓ cup cold vegetable shortening
- 8–10 tablespoons ice water

CARAMEL FILLING

- ½ cup bacon, uncooked and roughly chopped
- 1 cup granulated sugar
- 6 tablespoons butter, melted
- 4 ounces heavy cream, at room temperature
- 1 teaspoon coarse sea salt

PIE EXTRAS

- ½ cup dark chocolate chips
- 1 teaspoon bacon grease
- 2 teaspoons sea salt for dusting whipped cream (optional)

1 To make the pie crust, combine flour, salt, and sugar in a food processor. Pulse a couple of times then add in the butter and shortening. Pulse until pea-sized clumps form.

2 Slowly pulse in the water until the dough begins to form a ball. Roll the dough into a ball on a floured surface, divide in 2, then flatten into 2 disks. Wrap in plastic wrap and refrigerate for 30 minutes.

3 For the caramel filling, cook the chopped bacon in a medium saucepan just until crispy. Add in the sugar and stir constantly to avoid burning.

4 Cook until the sugar is melted and amber in color. Carefully add the butter to avoid rapid bubbling. Stir constantly until the butter is incorporated, 1–2 minutes.

5 Slowly stir in the whipping cream and boil for 1 minute. Stir in the sea salt, remove from heat and let cool.

6 Preheat oven to 400°F.

7 Working with 1 section at a time, remove the dough from the fridge. Roll dough to ⅛" thickness on a floured surface, then cut into 3" circles. Repeat with the other half of the dough until you have 24 circles. Place 1 circle in each cup of a mini–muffin pan and push down to form a cup. Bake for 7–10 minutes until the crust is golden brown. Cool completely.

8 Microwave the chocolate and 1 teaspoon bacon grease in a bowl for 30-second intervals until melted. Dip the rim of each pie in the chocolate, and then dust with sea salt. Let the chocolate cool. Fill each cup halfway with the caramel. Serve warm or let cool completely.

CHAPTER 7

Swine and Wine

When you think about bacon, one of the last things you associate with it is probably red wine. Believe it or not, red wine is what led to the creation of Baconfreak.com! In 2000, Rocco started a new online business dedicated to corporate deliveries of wines, wine clubs, and wine gift baskets. To promote the business, sell wine clubs, and have some fun while doing so, Rocco began hosting wine dinners. As an Italian who grew up in the kitchen, Rocco found his casual approach to wine drinking and wine tastings clashed with the chefs and their overly fussy approach.

The chefs insisted that specific foods must be paired with very specific wines, based on the region where it was grown and the varietal. Rocco disagreed with the notion that wine pairings need to be so strict and by the book, and recognized that most people attending the wine dinners didn't have that sophisticated of a palate. Rocco's focus was on why he likes a particular wine, and to match those wines to the foods he loves eating.

He asked the chefs a simple question: Why not pair one flavor found in the wine with a food that has a similar flavor? To highlight the peppery flavor of red wines, like Syrah and Pinot noir, Rocco created a new pairing: bruschetta on thick ciabatta bread with fresh tomatoes, garlic, basil, olive oil, and peppered bacon, paired with a very peppery Syrah.

Suddenly, people were really getting it. Pepper in the wine and pepper in the food. It was so obvious, so simple, and so delicious! Bacon hadn't exploded in popularity yet, but the conversation turned to bacon and was fueled by everyone's mutual love of meat candy. It was the least sophisticated wine dinner he'd had yet, but it was definitely the most fun.

Having found his winning combination, Rocco hosted more events, pairing simple bacon flavors with wine. Eventually, he noticed that, in addition to the usual oenophiles who attended his events, he was beginning to attract a wider range of wine consumers, including more men and "everyday Joes" whom Rocco affectionately referred to as "Bubbas." Rocco had never met so many Bubbas at a wine dinner, and this memorable event would eventually inspire the "Baby Bubba" line of bacon.

One night at an event, a guest affectionately proclaimed, "Here comes the Bacon Freak!" and something clicked in Rocco's mind. Baconfreak.com was born that night, and swine and wine were never the same. Soon the popularity of bacon surpassed the popularity of wine, and the "Bacon Is Meat Candy" Bacon Club was born.

When it comes to wine pairings, Rocco adheres to the following basic principles:

BACON BITS
Bacon-flavored bourbon and vodka can be found at your local liquor store.

* Drink the cheapest wine you like.
* Drink the most expensive bottle first.
* A great bottle of wine in bad company is a bad bottle of wine.
* A bad bottle of wine in good company is a great bottle of wine.
* Focus on flavors in the wine and why you like that wine, not the varietal.
* Don't be a "wine snob." Just be a Bubba and have fun!

Pork: The Other Bubbly Wine Meat

Although Rocco's bacon and wine dinners are a thing of the past, lucky Angelenos can experience bacon and wine pairings at a wine shop in Santa Monica, owned by wine expert Roberto Rogness. Roberto has been Wine Expo's general manager and wine director since 1993.

Wine Expo, Santa Monica's premier wine shop since 1993, primarily sells European wines with a strong emphasis on Italian wines, Spanish wines, and French champagne, a large majority of which is sourced on buying trips to these countries. Wine Expo's Bacon + Bubbly = Bliss events, which began as a bacon and champagne tasting among friends sixteen years ago on New Year's morning, are now held on the second Friday and Saturday of every month.

At the core of the success of the Bacon + Bubbly = Bliss events is the idea that bacon and sparkling wine complement each other perfectly. "The best thing to pair with bacon is champagne and other sparkling wine," says Roberto. "You want something that is dry, acidic, and that has bubbles. These three things are key. Fat and bubbles complement each other. The crisp acidity of sparkling wine cuts through the fatty flavor of the bacon and tones down its fat and saltiness. This refreshes the palate and makes you want to eat more."

Each Bacon + Bubbly = Bliss event serves up five select varieties of Bacon Freak bacon, along with five distinctly different sparkling wines. The bacon is served on a platter with nuts, olives, bread, and crackers, and guests are encouraged to mix and match to find their own favorite pairing. Says Roberto, "We don't dictate to people which bacon to eat with which champagne. It's up to them to figure out which is a great pairing. Someone might dig the Cajun bacon with the really dry champagne. Or someone might enjoy the same bacon with a rosé." Some examples of wines served at past events include:

* Laherte Grand Brut Tradition à Chavot la Champagne

BACON BITS
According to Google Maps, the following states have a town called "Bacon": Idaho, Indiana, Missouri, Ohio, Texas, and Washington.

* Bouquin-Dupont Fils Grand Cru Blanc de Blancs, Avize
* Lenoble Brut Cuvée Intense, Damery la Champagne
* Trouillard Brut Extra Sélection à Hautvillers
* Ricci Curbastro Franciacorta Rosé Brut, Lombardia

Not sure which sparkling wine to try with a specific dish or a particular bacon? Visit a local winery or wine shop to get some recommendations from the people who know good wines. If you're shopping at your local grocery store, just keep in mind that it needs to be dry, acidic, and bubbly. Look for key words like *Brut* and *Extra Brut*. And don't worry about ending up with a stinker.

Nonsparkling Red and White Wines

Before discussing which red and white wines to pair with foods of the porcine persuasion, it's important to remember that just because you try a wine and don't like it on its own, doesn't mean you wouldn't love it if it were paired with the right food.

Here are some of Roberto's general recommendations to keep in mind when on the hunt for red or white wines to pair with bacon and bacon dishes:

* Acidity in the wine is key. Bacon already has all the fat and salt you need. So a fairly sharp, acidic wine cuts the flavor of the fat.
* Choose wines that are a little bit restrained so you can taste all the different flavors. Earthiness is a definite characteristic of wines that are not too ripe so that you can taste other flavors beside the sugar.
* Drink wine while eating food to find that binary flavor bomb, where 1 + 1 = 5.
* Drink wine that tastes like wine. Wine shouldn't taste like blueberry pancake syrup!
* Focus on the flavors in the wine, not the type of wine.
* Try varietals you wouldn't normally try.
* And, lastly, remember: A good bottle of wine doesn't have to be expensive.

Cheers to that!

Look for Roberto's Wine Picks on select recipes. To see Baconfreak.com's selections of preferred wines for swine and wine pairings, visit our Swine and Wine webpage.

Swine and Suds

Barley beverages and salty swine: it's no surprise that America's favorite beverage pairs oh so perfectly with America's favorite meat candy. Bacon's versatility and its ability to enhance any food parallel the unique versatility and complexity of beer. It could be argued that, compared to wine, beer is a much more food-friendly beverage because there are so many more ingredients to play with. All beers include some of these basic ingredients that are used to brew beer, including hops, barley, malt, wheat, and yeast. Compare this to the winemaker who only works with grapes!

Today's brewmasters are taking their beers into new dimensions by adding a plethora of different ingredients, like pumpkin, coconut, raspberry, cherry, orange peel, lemon zest, licorice, hazelnuts, chocolate, spices, and even "wine" grapes, including Syrah, Cabernet Sauvignon, and Riesling! When it comes to beer, the possibilities are proving to be endless.

The craft beer movement has reached epic proportions as new microbreweries are popping up in small towns and major cities across the United States. Well-established microbreweries continue to expand and thrive. And some microbreweries have done so well they've been bought out by macrobreweries, the musical equivalent of your favorite indie band signing with a major label. From your corner liquor mart to stores like BevMo and Total Wine, there are countless beers to choose from when pairing beer with your beloved bacon.

As with Swine and Wine, we don't believe there should be strict rules when it comes to pairing Suds and Swine. If you're an avid beer drinker, you're probably going to drink your favorite beer with whatever you want, anyway. And to that, we raise a pint and wish you "Cheers." But, as with wine, we believe that it's important to try new things and branch out from what is familiar to you.

You might be surprised by what you discover and might soon replace your "tried-and-true" brews with a newfound favorite. So don't be afraid to venture out into the world of beers you've never tried before. Select several different varieties and throw an impromptu tasting party.

We asked our local brewmaster for his input on the best beers to pair with bacon. Brew captain Chris Enegren started Enegren Brewing Co. (www.enegrenbrewing.com) in the dorm rooms of Loyola Marymount University where he brewed his first batches on a friend's on-campus apartment stove.

ENEGREN'S PICKS

The Big Meat Rauchbier

Rauchbier is made with malt that has been dried over open beechwood flames. This imparts a distinctive, smoky flavor to the finished product. The flavor is so similar to the hickory flavor of bacon that rauchbier is sometimes referred to as "bacon beer." *Rauchbier* means "smoke beer" in German, and at one time, all beers in Germany were technically "rauchbier" because of the traditional kiln method of drying the malt over open fires.

Those who have tried rauchbier tend to either love it or hate it. But the mistake the haters have made is not pairing this beer with food. The robust, smoky tang of rauchbier may be overwhelming to the palate when consumed alone. However, it stands up well to the strong flavors of smoked meats, like bacon, ham, pork,

sausage, and smoked cheeses, like gouda, mozzarella, and provolone. It also goes well with foods cooked on the barbecue, and rauchbier can even be used as a marinade.

The Big Meat is Enegren's rauchbier-style beer. The beechwood-smoked malt adds a distinctive smokiness to the brew, similar to what you find in a good BBQ. At 7.6 percent alcohol by volume (ABV), this beer is bigger than a traditional rauchbier, befitting its name. To balance out the smokiness, the beer is brewed with Munich and caramel malts for a malty and caramel flavor that goes down smooth and is the perfect pairing for smoked meats, especially smoky bacon.

Valkyrie Altbier

Enegren also recommends pairing bacon with altbier. Enegren's Valkyrie altbier is brewed following the traditions of one of the oldest beer styles in Germany. The name *altbier* means "old beer" in German, referring to the old style of prelager beer.

Enegren's version of altbier is a little stronger, maltier, and darker than most of its German counterparts. Brewed with dark Munich and Pilsner malts, imported from Germany, Valkyrie has a smooth, toasty, caramel taste, with hints of chocolate and sweetness, balanced by a hefty dose of German noble hops. The result is a highly drinkable beer that is not too dark and not too heavy, perfect for pairing with meat. Its toasty, caramel notes will bring out the caramelized flavors found in barbecued foods, especially bacon.

IPAs

Although there are many IPAs (India Pale Ales) on Enegren's beer list, in general, the brewmeisters at Enegren recommend that you stay away from IPAs when pairing beer with bacon. These overly hoppy beers compete too much with the rich, hearty flavors found in bacon dishes and tend to overload the palate. If you have your heart set on IPA experimentation, start with an IPA that ranks lower on the IBU (international bitterness units) scale, indicating the level of bitterness. If you're a devoted IPA fan, continue to be a rebel and drink whatever you want.

ROBERTO'S TOP THREE BEER PICKS

Our friend Roberto offers up his Top 3 Beer Picks for pairing with bacon:

1. Flanders red ale (also known as Flemish red ale)
The classic beer and bacon pairing is Flanders red ale. These are Belgian ales that are fermented in large oak barrels with lactobacillis yeast, which is the type of yeast that makes

BACON BITS

Did you know that bacon has its own patron saint? Saint Anthony the Abbott is the patron saint of swine herders, pigs, and butchers.

yogurt. This imparts a bright, slightly sour and acidic flavor to the beer, reminiscent of fruits like cranberry, red currant, and plums. Because they are inoculated with a different yeast and aged in oak barrels, this gives them a tangy flavor that cuts through the maltiness and makes them very refreshing. They pair exceptionally well with bacon, sausage, and charcuterie. Flanders red ales are called the "red wine" of the beer world because of the presence of tannins in the beer and because of the barrel-aging process.

2. Witbier (also called witte ale, white ale, wheat ale, or bière blanche)

Witbier pairs well with bacon for the same reasons sparkling wines do. It is very refreshing on the palate and cuts right through the rich, fatty flavor of bacon. Witbiers are usually brewed with coriander, orange peel, or citrus of some sort, and contain a large proportion of wheat, relative to barley. Witbiers go down easily, due to their crispness, freshness, bright citrus flavor, and slight carbonation.

3. Stouts and Porters

Stouts and porters have richness, some effervescence, and some acidity, and go well with bacon, sausage, and other smoked meats. Avoid overly heavy stouts and porters. A good indicator of heaviness is alcohol content. A stout or porter with high alcohol content might be too robust and could overpower the flavor of the food. A smoky porter or stout will enhance and complement the smoky flavor of bacon. A chocolate porter or stout will taste amazing with any sort of chocolate dessert. A nitro stout guarantees a silky-smooth finish, and milk stouts are also known for their creamy, smooth flavor.

OTHER PICKS

Maple Beer

If you've ever drizzled maple syrup over your crispy bacon strips, consider pairing a maple beer with bacon. From tree tap to bar tap, the process of making maple beers is difficult to perfect. Crafting a maple beer with maple flavor involves a delicate balance of just the right amounts of maple sap, maple syrup, grains, hops, yeast, and barrel aging. Maple beers run the gamut of flavors from smoky to sweet. Some examples to look for include Voodoo Doughnut Maple Bacon Ale by Rogue Ales, Maple Pecan Porter by Sam Adams, Autumn Maple by The Bruery, Maple Bacon

BACON BITS

Which gender would you guess loves bacon more—men or women? Well, according to a survey by Livestrong.com, more women than men reported eating bacon on a monthly basis.

Coffee Porter by Funky Buddha Brewery, and Big Leaf Maple Autumn Red by Anchor Brewing.

Bière de Champagne (also called Bière Brut) Bière de champagne, or champagne beer, is one of the newest additions to the world of craft beer. Primarily made in Belgium, it's a light, sparkling beer that looks and tastes just like champagne. During the brewing process, champagne yeast is used in place of regular beer yeast. This gives it the carbonation and taste that recall the fizz and flavor of real sparkling wine. Some of these beers are actually cave-aged alongside real champagne bottles in the Champagne region of France and subjected to the *method de champenoise*, which is the method for removing yeast from the bottle. The first and most famous champagne beer, Deus Brut des Flandres, or DeuS for short, is brewed in Buggenhout, Belgium by Brouwerij Bosteels. Although it is often consumed as an apéritif, we like it with bacon for the same reasons we pair bacon with sparkling wine. Its effervescence and light flavor cut through the heavy fattiness of bacon and refresh the palate.

Cider and Swine

Which of these items is the most trendy: bacon, food trucks, craft beer, or hard cider? Well, consider these statistics from the *Hard Cider Journal*. In 2012, the hard cider market experienced a 90 percent growth in sales. In 2013, it grew 89 percent and in 2014, it grew 71 percent. Compare this to the less than 3 percent growth in wine and beer sales, and you've got a pretty good indication that the answer to our question is hard cider.

Today's social drinkers are experimenting with hard cider much as they did with craft beer years ago. According to Angry Orchard, the iconic hard cider company, cider is attracting beer and wine drinkers looking for a refreshing alternative. Traditionally, ciders have been compared more to beer, based on how they're served and similar ABV (typically around 5 percent). But the actual cidermaking process is more closely associated with wine.

Angry Orchard Crisp Apple Hard Cider is the perfect companion to bacon for a number of reasons. The cider is made with a mix of culinary and traditional cider apples. With a bacon and cider pairing, the acidity from the culinary apples cuts through the inherent rich, salty, smoky flavor of the bacon, while the complexity of the traditional cider apples complements some of the heavier bacon flavors. The carbonization achieves two things: Its slight effervescence cuts through the fattiness, and refreshes and cleanses the palate in preparation for the next bite. Again, there are no hard-and-fast rules for pairing cider with bacon; it's up to you to experiment and find your perfect pairing.

What Would You Give Up for Bacon?

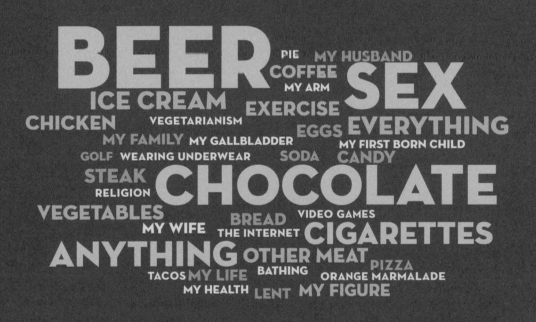

CHAPTER 8

Putting Bacon on the Map

On the Move with Bacon

BACON FOOD TRUCKS

The food truck trend is just as sizzling as the bacon trend. New food trucks are popping up everywhere, and food truck events—where many trucks gather in one location—are becoming popular in urban centers and even in some suburban enclaves. Unlike the bacon trend, there is a downside to the food truck trend: Some trucks are disappearing almost as quickly as they appear. But several well-known trucks (and some not-so-well-known) are proof that bacon and food trucks haven't nearly jumped the shark yet.

BACON BABES
Indianapolis, Indiana
http://www.baconbabesfoodtruck.com
The Bacon Babes food truck describes itself as an "innovative food truck making bacon recipes with grass-fed, cage-free & nitrate-free ingredients." A lady pig in a green cocktail dress adorns the truck logo. Owner Staci R. Fahlsing creates family-friendly comfort food made with quality ingredients. The Bacon Bison Burger includes a grass-fed bison patty, nitrate-free bacon made from pastured pigs, and bacon aioli. It's served on a homemade bun from Scholar's Inn Bakery. The Grilled Peanut Butter Sandwich is smothered in 100 percent maple syrup, peanut butter, and crispy bacon strips. And the Armadillo Eggs are jalapeños stuffed with feta and cream cheese, covered in ground bison and wrapped in bacon. They're creamy and spicy on the inside, crispy and sizzling on the outside.

BACON BACON
San Francisco, California
http://www.baconbaconsf.com
Perhaps the most popular bacon food truck of them all, Bacon Bacon traveled a bumpy road to success. In 2012 the truck caught on fire. In 2013, complaints from suspected vegetarian neighbors threatened to temporarily shut down Bacon Bacon's café location. The issue? You won't believe it, but people were complaining about the overwhelming scent of bacon. We know. People are crazy. . . . But fan support has been strong, and this popular truck serves up a bounty of bacon items, like the Bacon Grilled Cheese, made with bacon and bacon jam, and the California Bacon BBQ Burrito, made with pulled pork, crispy pork belly, and bacon. Even the fries have pork belly trimmings!

BACON MANIA

Sacramento and Orange County, California

http://baconmaniatruck.com

Another California favorite, Bacon MANia has two trucks, one serving the Sacramento area, and another that visits Orange County. Bacon MANia describes its food as "unabashedly American, unapologetic man-food." However, we're pretty sure women will want to devour these dishes, too. Menu items include Bacon MANia's award-winning Mac'N Bac'n, named "America's Best" by *Travel & Leisure* magazine. It's made with sharp cheddar, hickory-smoked bacon, and a spicy chipotle sauce, and you can get it on fries or on a bacon-wrapped, all-beef hot dog.

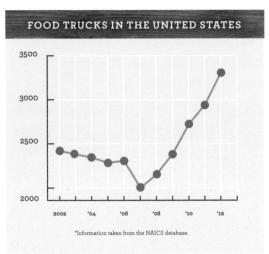

FOOD TRUCKS IN THE UNITED STATES

*Information taken from the NAICS database.

BACON NATION

Nashville, Tennessee

http://www.baconnationnash.com

"Life, liberty and the pursuit of bacon" is Bacon Nation's mantra. Established in 2013, Bacon Nation promises to deliver Nashville's favorite bacon menu. Owners Justin Roman and Cory Vinson started the truck because of their love of bacon and their desire to be self-employed. What better way to do that than by spreading the bacon love? Their signature menu item, the Dynamite Burger, has a 50 percent ground bacon/50 percent beef patty topped with grilled onions, jalapeños, and white queso. The Double Bypass consists of two ⅓-pound 50/50 patties served between two bacon grilled cheese sandwiches. For dessert, you can indulge in crispy bacon strips covered in white chocolate. The Ultimate BLT was recently named one of the "Top 8" bacon dishes to try in Nashville.

BACON N ED'S

Reston, Virginia

https://www.facebook.com/BaconNEds

Created by chef/owner Ed Hardy and Sous Chef/Partner Evan Henris, Bacon N Ed's is a mobile gourmet kitchen with lots of bacon on the menu. The chefs believe that dull food is bad food; that no food moment should be wasted; that each bite should have intense flavor, invoke nostalgia, and spark emotion. They smoke their bacon in-house and use local, sustainable ingredients whenever possible. The house-made bacon is on their classic BLT, the Fried Chicken Bahn-Mi, and their Bacon N Herb Fries. For those looking for a more upscale bacon dining experience, Bacon N Ed's mobile chef's table serves up exclusive four-course tasting menus for four to eight people.

BLONDIE'S BACON CREATIONS

Las Vegas, Nevada

http://www.blondiesbaconcreations.com

Kelly (aka Blondie) traveled a bumpy road to food truck success. This single mother of two was inspired to start her own food truck after catering a bacon-themed bachelorette party for a friend, complete with a bacon tower. Now she's bringing the bacon to the people of Las Vegas and living by the belief that "Bacon makes everything better." In addition to standards, like the BLT and the bacon melt, the menu includes unique items like Bacon and Avocado Egg Rolls, served with cilantro sauce. And the Bacon Tater

BACON BITS

The phrase *when pigs fly* is thought to be an old Scottish proverb. It was made popular in Lewis Carroll's *Alice in Wonderland*, when the Duchess tells Alice that she has as much right to think as "pigs have to fly."

Balls are bite-sized bits of pure comfort food. These bacon-infused potato balls are stuffed with cheese, rolled in panko, deep-fried, and served with a lemon sour cream dipping sauce.

I LOVE BACON TRUCK

Huntsville, Alabama

http://www.ilovebacontruck.com

The I Love Bacon Truck promises food "made from the best stuff on earth." For a mere $2.75, you can add double bacon to any menu item. All the menu items offered by this food truck are musically themed. The Carlos Santana is a riff on the national sandwich of Uruguay—the chiveto. It's loaded with flank steak, bacon, ham, fried egg, Swiss cheese, lettuce, tomato, and smoky mayo. The Public Enemy Mac & Cheese has creamy penne pasta and is topped with crumbled bacon, diced jalapeños, and queso. You can also enjoy the spicy mac & cheese stuffed in the Notorious B.I.G., a carb bomb of a grilled cheese sandwich. And the Tenacious D nachos feature braised pork belly, caramelized onions, and sriracha sour cream.

MAKIN' BACON

Saginaw, Michigan

https://www.facebook.com/makinbacontruck

Owners Nicholas and Barbara Christophilopoulos are thrilled to bring Saginaw, Michigan a rolling celebration of the glorious gastronomical delight that is bacon. The truck features items like the

Mexicali Breakfast Burrito with either bacon or chorizo, the Pulled Pork Street Bowl, the Makin' Bacon Street Brat, a five-cheese Bacon Mac and Cheese, and desserts like Chocolate-Covered Bacon and Bacon Toffee!

MASTERBACON

Concord, North Carolina

http://www.masterbacon.com

MasterBacon isn't just a food truck: It's a Bacon Response Unit (B.R.U. for short). Simply dial **EAT BACON on your cell phone if ever you find yourself suffering from a lunch or dinner bereft of your beloved bacon. Owner and executive chef Greg Helmandollar worked for fifteen years at various restaurants, including Mickey & Mooch, Providence Bistro, and Union Street Bistro. Greg and his father-in-law, who helps manage the truck, are both military veterans, and give back to their community by helping disabled veterans. Their signature item, the Bacon Explosion Burger, consists of a bacon weave, a layer of black angus beef, a layer of their signature smoked gouda spread, a layer of smoked pulled pork belly, and jalapeño slices. It's then rolled up like a pinwheel, roasted in the oven, sliced, and served on a bun with fresh spinach and tomatoes. Their Buffalo Bombs are hard-boiled eggs, wrapped in bacon, then tossed in buffalo sauce. And their Bacon-Wrapped Deep-Fried Cheesecake is the ultimate dessert.

SKILLET STREET FOOD

Seattle, Washington

http://skilletstreetfood.com

Launched in 2007, Skillet Street Food was one of the pioneers of the upscale street food movement that has been sweeping the country. The original street food business, which emerged from a vintage Airstream trailer, now includes three restaurants, three food trucks, and a line of food products. The Skillet Airstream has become synonymous with amazing street food. Skillet redefines modern American food: approachable, upscale, prepared with classic techniques, and using local and seasonal ingredients. Skillet Bacon Spreads, or "Bacon Jam," was introduced in 2010 in response to customers who were pleading for the smoky, tangy, savory, sweet spread topping the famous Skillet burger. The Skillet burger includes grass-fed beef, arugula,

blue cheese, and Brie cheese, and is slathered with Skillet's signature spread and served on a brioche bun.

SUM PIG FOOD
Philadelphia, Pennsylvania
http://www.sumpigfoodtruck.com
Sum refers to the well-traveled youths of owners Jessica, a professional racecar driver, and Steve, the son of a famous radio personality. Influenced by their global travels, recipes composed of fresh, locally sourced (whenever possible) ingredients, paired with heartfelt cooking, are the foundation of Sum Pig. *Pig* not only refers to their delicious smoked meats, but their generous portion sizes as well. Pigging out is strongly encouraged! Their menu includes items like the Peanut Butter & Bacon, with thick-cut Applewood-smoked bacon served on Texas toast and torched to perfection, and the Bacon Bleu, a smoked pork sandwich with bacon, gorgonzola cheese, and their signature Carolina BBQ sauce.

THE BACON BOSS
Tampa Bay, Florida
https://www.facebook.
comTheBaconBossFoodTruck
With a slogan of "Keep your friends close and your bacon closer," the Bacon Boss food truck is where the people of Tampa Bay get their bacon fix. The Bacon Boss is the brainchild of

Joshua Norland, who decided to quit his day job and pursue his dream of being his own boss. He came up with the bacon theme when trying to determine which food appeals to almost everyone. With the help of graphic designer Dave Velez, the Mafia mascot was born. Josh's wife Christy worked on creating the names for the menu items. Their meatcentric menu is mobster-themed, with items like the Mafioso Burger, the Conway Mac and Cheese, and the Jimmy Hoffa Hot Dog.

THE BACON TRUCK
Boston, Massachusetts
http://www.bostonbacontruck.com
Truck owners Sam and JJ have been friends since high school, but bacon lovers since birth. After finishing college, they wanted to create a truck with a menu focused on the single greatest food known to mankind: bacon. They hold these truths

to be self-evident, that all foods are not created equal, that bacon is superior to every other food on the planet. Menu items include the hangover sandwich, made with bacon, bacon scallion hash, Havarti and cheddar cheeses, and a fried egg. Or there's the bacon and bourbon BBQ pulled pork sliders. For dessert, there's always Nutella® bacon and chocolate bacon truffles.

THE BLT TRUCK

Los Angeles, California

http://theblttruck.com

The BLT Truck is Marcona Restaurant's mobile vendor, bringing fresh, classic BLTs and a handful of clever variations on the BLT to the people of Los Angeles. Featuring a minimalist menu with only five items (including a vegan option), this new addition to the bacon food truck scene serves five different BLTs on its signature "Rockenwagner" pretzel rolls. The classic BLT includes tarragon aioli, and the breakfast BLT has ketchup, sharp cheddar, and a fried egg. You don't want to know what the vegan version includes . . .

Bacon Festivals: The Communal Congress of Carnal Consumption

Like the Comic-Con of the nerd world, bacon fans flock to bacon festivals to celebrate their love of bacon with fellow bacon freaks. But unlike Comic-Con, tickets to bacon festivals don't sell out in two seconds, and just about every state has its own event. From Juneau, Alaska, to St. Augustine, Florida, bacon festivals are equally appealing to hipsters and hicks when the goal is simply to eat a ton of bacon. There's just something about bacon that makes people want to pork out together, like the bacon gluttons they are. Because at a bacon festival, not only is bacon gluttony something to celebrate, but it's something that is often rewarded.

The proliferation of bacon festivals across the United States reflects bacon's increasing popularity. Consider these attendance stats for the One Bacon Festival to Rule Them All: the Blue Ribbon Bacon Festival, held in Des Moines, Iowa. In 2008, there were 175 total participants and since then, this number has almost doubled annually. In 2014, 12,000 tickets sold out in forty-two minutes. In 2015, a total of 14,000 people attended and ate a whopping 20,000 pounds of bacon, served in ninety-four different drinks and dishes! Bacon lovers from forty-one different states and seven countries attended.

Although events vary from festival to festival, they generally include samplings of a plethora of bacon dishes, bacon desserts, bacon cocktails, and beers from various food vendors whose primary objective is to stuff you silly. Bacon lectures, bacon swag bags, bacon eating contests, bacon pageants, bacon costumes, live music, bacon weddings, and, in general, a whole lotta bacon merriment are on the "menu."

Brooks Reynolds, founder of the Blue Ribbon Bacon Festival events, describes the "recipe for success" of the BRBF: "The Blue Ribbon Bacon Festival is a great way for folks to try a wide variety of bacon. We have the largest bacon showcase of any bacon festival in the world. From Bacon Gelato, Korean Tacos, Elvis-Inspired Pizza, Bacon-Wrapped Ribs, Maple Doughnuts and, one of my favorites, the Bacon Explosion. We have lectures at our events, like the History of Bacon, the Science of Bacon, Dry-Cured versus Wet-Cured Bacon. You'll see people dressed as Kevin Bacon, Bacon Zombies, Icelandic Bacon Vikings, and a whole lot of Bacon Elvises, all wanting to share in Bacon Fellowship! Bacon Fellowship is demonstrating a shared passion to improve the enjoyment of all things bacon through education, recognition, advocacy, and research."

It is perhaps this sense of community that has led to the popularity of the "bacon wedding." For some people, it's not enough to attend a bacon festival; they want to get married there, too. Adam Poch, the *Big Brother* TV show contestant who is reality TV's greatest bacon champion, served as officiant at two bacon-themed weddings that took place at the 2014 Blue Ribbon Bacon Festival.

Bacon festivals are not only a way to entertain, educate, feed, and marry folks, most importantly, they are opportunities to give back to the communities where they take place. Brooks says, "With all of the events that we have done since 2008, the Iowa Bacon Board, Blue Ribbon Bacon Festival events, and the Iceland Bacon Board have helped raise over $200,000 for non-for-profits in Iowa, Iceland, Colorado, and Wisconsin." And that's something any bacon fan in a white, polyester Elvis costume can feel proud about.

BACON BITS

The first known bacon costume was worn in 1894 by a man named George J. Nicholls. He won first prize and forty guineas at the Covent Garden Fancy Dress Ball in London, England.

The Bacon Takedowns: "Master Chef" Meets Bacon Fest

http://thetakedowns.com

Another community-fueled bacon event is the "Bacon Takedown." The Takedown is an awesome conceptual food event, held in venues all over the country that has taken the culinary world by storm. As part food festival and part competition, the premise behind the event is simple. Set the theme of the event. Like, bacon. Next, invite home cooks to compete. Supply them with the sponsored ingredient. Each competitor cooks up enough food to feed a hungry, lucky crowd of ticket holders, who pay about $15 to sample dozens of dishes. Attendees vote on their favorites, and the winner takes home a ton of awesome prizes and, most importantly, the sought-after title of Takedown Champion.

The mastermind behind the Takedowns is Matt Timms, who's been organizing the Takedowns for over a decade. He wanted to create a food competition with a casual party atmosphere and without any restrictive rules. The Takedowns are, in essence, a communal celebration of good food and the people who love it. Paying homage to the main ingredient is also key.

Adrian Ashby was the winner of the October 2014 Brooklyn Bacon Takedown with his Bacon Hash recipe. We asked Adrian what it's like to participate in a Takedown, and he had this to say: "Participating in the Brooklyn Bacon Takedown was awesome! It's a mad rush of people coming up to you, wanting to try your dish, and seeing their reactions is awesome when you know you made something great, especially when folks come back for seconds, thirds, or more. It was an awesome feeling hearing my name called as the winner!"

Check out this wonderfully fatty, fully fleshed-out list of bacon festivals that were held in 2015. Who knows what the future holds for the almighty Bacon Fest? We're hungry with anticipation.

ALFERD PACKER BACON PARTY
Littlecon, Colorado
http://alferdpackerbaconparty.com

AMERICA LOVES BACON FESTIVAL
Knoxville, Tennessee
http://americalovesbacon.com

AMERICA LOVES BACON FESTIVAL
Phoenix/Scottsdale, Arizona
http://americalovesbacon.com

ANCHORAGE BEER AND BACON FESTIVAL
Anchorage, Alaska
http://www.anchoragenightout.com

ARIZONA BACON FEST
Tucson, Arizona
http://www.arizonabaconfest.net

BACONALOOZA
Victoria, British Columbia, Canada
http://www.baconalooza.com

BACON & BARRELS
Solvang, California
San Diego, California
http://www.baconandbarrels.com

BACON AND BEER CLASSIC
Chicago, Illinois
http://www.baconandbeerclassic.com

BACON AND BEER CLASSIC
Indianapolis, Indiana
http://www.baconandbeerclassic.com

BACON AND BEER CLASSIC
Minneapolis, Minnesota
http://www.baconandbeerclassic.com

BACON AND BEER CLASSIC
New York, New York
http://www.baconandbeerclassic.com

BACON AND BEER CLASSIC
Philadelphia, Pennsylvania
http://www.baconandbeerclassic.com

BACON AND BEER CLASSIC
San Jose, California
http://www.baconandbeerclassic.com

BACON & BEER CLASSIC
Seattle, Washington
http://www.baconandbeerclassic.com

BACON BITS

In 2011, the record for the world's largest BLT was broken by the St. Louis restaurant called Iron Barley. Iron Barley's BLT included 600 pounds of bacon, 440 pounds of bread, 550 pounds of tomatoes, 220 heads of iceberg lettuce, and 60 gallons of mayo, and measured 224 feet long!

BACON & BEER FESTIVAL
Fargo, North Dakota
http://baconandbeerfargo.com

BACON AND BOURBON FESTIVAL
Charleston, South Carolina
http://www.baconandbourbonsc.com

BACON AND BREWFEST
Tuscaloosa, Alabama
http://953thebear.com/ALBaconBrewfest

BACON BASH TEXAS
Cranfills Gap, Texas
http://www.baconbashtexas.com

BACON, BREW & BBQ FEST
Sun Prairie, Wisconsin
http://www.bbbfest.com

BACON FEST
Kettering, Ohio
http://www.fraze.com/bacon-fest-2015

BACON FEST
Kansas City, Missouri
http://www.baconfestkc.com

BACONFEST ATL
Atlanta, Georgia
https://www.facebook.com/BaconfestATL

BACONFEST CHICAGO
Chicago, Illinois
http://baconfestchicago.com

BACONFEST MONMOUTH
Monmouth, Illinois
https://www.facebook.comBaconFestMonmouth

BACONFEST VA
Roanoke, Virginia
http://www.baconfestva.com

BEER & BACON FESTIVAL

Cary, North Carolina

http://www.beerandbacon.com

BEER & BACON FESTIVAL

Woodbridge, Virginia

http://www.beerandbacon.com/woodbridge

BEER BACON MUSIC

Frederick, Maryland

http://beerbaconmusic.com

BEER, BACON AND MUSIC FESTIVAL

Hilton Head Island, South Carolina

http://www.hiltonheadisland.com

BEER, BOURBON AND BACON FESTIVAL

Rhinebeck, New York

http://www.beerbourbonbacon.com

BIG BACON BONANZA

Davenport, Iowa

http://www.visitquadcities.com

BIG BITE BACON FEST

Long Beach, California

http://bigbiteevents.com

BLUE RIBBON BACON FEST

Des Moines, Iowa

http://blueribbonbaconfestival.com

CAVE SPRING BACON FEST

Cave Spring, Georgia

https://www.facebook.com/CaveSpringBaconFest

CEDAR VALLEY BACON FEST

Waterloo, Iowa

http://cedarvalleybaconfest.com

DALLAS BACON FESTIVAL

Dallas, Texas

http://www.baconrally.com

DELRAY BEACH BACON AND BOURBON FESTIVAL

Delray Beach, Florida

http://delraybaconandbourbonfest.com

DEWEY BEACH BACON FEST

Dewey Beach, Delaware

http://www.idewey.com

DUBUQUE AREA BACON FEST

Dubuque, Iowa

https://www.facebook.comDubuqueArea
Baconfest

GREAT BIG BACON PICNIC

Brooklyn, New York

http://greatbigbacon.com

GREAT SASKATCHEWAN BACON FESTIVAL

Saskatchewan, Kipling, Canada

http://www.baconfestival.ca

HEAVY SEAS BACON & BEER FESTIVAL
Halethrope, Maryland
http://www.hsbeer.com

HOGS FOR THE CAUSE 2015
New Orleans, Louisiana
http://www.hogsforthecause.org

HORMEL BLACK LABEL BACON FEST
San Diego, California
http://www.sdbaconfest.com

INDIANA BACON FESTIVAL OF CARROLL COUNTY
Delphi, Indiana
http://www.indianabaconfestival.com

JUNEAU BACONFEST
Juneau, Alaska
http://www.jahc.org

KEYSTONE BLUE RIBBON BACON TOUR
Keystone, Colorado
http://www.keystonefestivals.com/festivals/blue-ribbon-bacon-tour

BACON BITS
Indiana sells bacon-scented lottery tickets! Those who hold winning Hoosier tickets can collect up to $10,000 or a twenty-year supply of bacon.

LA BACON FEST
Los Angeles, California
http://labaconfest.com

LONG ISLAND BACON FEST
Coram, New York
https://www.cradleofaviation.org/plan_your_visit/event_calendar.html/event/2016/01/31/long-island-bacon-bash

MIDWEST BACONFEST
Park City, Kansas
http://www.midwestbaconfest.com

MONTEREY BACON FESTIVAL
Monterey, California
http://www.montereybaconfest.com

OMAHA BEER AND BACON FESTIVAL
Omaha, Nebraska
http://www.omahabeerandbacon.com

102.9 THE HOG MILWAUKEE BACONFEST
Milwaukee, Wisconsin
http://1029thehog.com/BACONFEST

PA BACONFEST
Easton, Pennsylvania
http://pabaconfest.com

PIGS ON PENN BACON FESTIVAL
York, Pennsylvania
http://www.downtownyorkpa.com/events/
baconfest

PORK DAYS, USA BACON FEST
Albion, Illinois
http://www.porkdaysusa.com

PORTLAND BOURBON AND BACON FESTIVAL
Portland, Oregon
http://portland.bourbonandbaconfest.com

REHOBOTH BEACH BACON FEST
Rehoboth Beach, Delaware
http://idewey.com/index.
cfm?ref=15200&ref2=397

REYKJAVIK BACON FESTIVAL
Reykjavik, Iceland
https://www.facebook.com/
ReykjavikBaconFestival

RIVER FALLS BACON BASH
River Falls, Wisconsin
http://www.riverfallsbaconbash.com

SACRAMENTO BACON FEST
Sacramento, California
http://www.baconfestsac.com

SAN MATEO BACON AND BREW FEST

San Mateo, California

http://www.sanmateochamber.org/bbf

SMITHFIELD BACON, BOURBON AND BEACH MUSIC FEST

Smithfield, Virginia

http://www.smithfieldvabaconfest.com

SOUTHWEST BACON FEST

Albuquerque, New Mexico

http://www.southwestbaconfest.com

THREE RIVERS CRAFT BREW AND BACON FESTIVAL

Kennewick, Washington

http://www.threeriversconventioncenter.com

ZINGERMAN'S CAMP BACON

Ann Arbor, Michigan

http://www.zingermanscampbacon.com

Around the World with Bacon

Americans aren't the only ones addicted to bacon. Bacon is beloved around the world, and it's just as much a staple in other cultures and countries as it is in the United States. Although we share a mutual love for bacon, bacon from other countries isn't going to look or taste like the bacon that we eat in the United States. Despite these differences, bacon's versatility and ability to make other foods better is universal. Traveling abroad shouldn't stop you from enjoying bacon, so here's what to expect when ordering bacon in other countries. Many of these varieties of bacon are available in the United States, so feel free to expand your bacon horizons and experiment with one of these tasty bacon variants.

WORLD PORK CONSUMPTION

Less ——————— More

*Data from UN Food and Agriculture Organization

Asia

LOP YUK Lop yuk or lap yuk is the Chinese version of bacon! It comes from the pork belly and is dry-cured and flavored with soy sauce, brown sugar, and various Asian spices. It is dryer and harder than U.S. bacon and can be found in Asian markets in 1"-thick slabs. It can be eaten on its own or used to flavor other dishes like stir-fries and noodle and rice dishes.

Australia and New Zealand

MIDDLE BACON Middle bacon comes from the side or loin. Common in Australia and New Zealand, middle bacon is sold in "rashers." Middle bacon includes the streaky, fatty section, along with the loin at one end. The texture and flavor therefore strike the "middle" ground between streaky bacon and back bacon.

Canada

Canadians eat "American" bacon and it is referred to as "bacon bacon." The term *Canadian bacon* is only used in the United States.

PEAMEAL BACON Peameal bacon is similar to back bacon and is made from lean, boneless pork loin with a very thin fat layer, trimmed to ⅛". It is sweet pickle–brined, unsmoked, and coated in cornmeal. It was traditionally coated in ground yellow peas, hence its name, but it has been coated in cornmeal since World War II. The purpose of the peameal was to help the brine set and extend its shelf life. It is similar to an American pork loin roast in taste

and appearance. Traditionally, it is glazed and roasted like U.S. pork tenderloin. It is also sliced and served in the Canadian version of a BLT and in Eggs Benedict.

Europe

AUSTRIA

TYROLEAN SPECK Bacon from the Tyrol region of Austria.

FRANCE

LARDONS The French version of the Italian lardo, lardons come from salt-cured, unsmoked fatback. They are used in food preparation and are also fried and added to dishes. Lardons are often used in French cuisine to prepare Julia Child's classic *Boeuf Bourguignon* and *Coq au Vin*. *Salade aux Lardons* is a salad where the leaves have wilted due to the addition of hot, crispy lardons.

LARD SALÉ Lard salé comes from the pork belly and is cured, with or without streaks of meat. It is similar to American salt pork.

GERMANY

BAUCHSPECK Bauchspeck is similar to U.S. bacon. It comes from the pork belly and is streaked with muscle and fat. It is dry-cured with salt, smoked with beechwood, and aged by air-drying. Also known as *durchwachsener speck*, it is usually sold in slabs that are sliced and diced then pan-fried after the rind is removed.

FRÜHSTÜCKSSPECK This bacon is similar to U.S. bacon and is typically eaten at breakfast.

BACON BITS

Kummerspeck is defined as excess weight gained from emotional overeating. In German, it literally means "grief bacon."

RÜCKENSPECK Fatback that is cured and smoked. It is rendered fresh into lard, or *schmalz*, and often eaten on bread, like butter. It is also used as a cooking fat for browning meat and onions and for frying potatoes.

SCHINKENSPECK *Schinken* means "ham" and *speck* means "bacon." Schinkenspeck is from the hip and is dry-cured, seasoned with juniper berries and other spices, and smoked. One traditional way of eating it is to serve it thinly sliced and uncooked on dark crusty bread with cheese. It is also eaten cooked and is sliced into strips and pan-fried.

SPECK: The German word for "bacon." Speck comes from the belly or the side and is dry-cured and heavily smoked. It can be rendered into lard or used to flavor other foods.

HUNGARY

GYPSY BACON A Hungarian delicacy, gypsy bacon is seasoned with garlic and paprika and is smoked. Also known as *Zigeunerspeck,* gypsy bacon is available in German or Hungarian delis and markets. It is traditionally cooked on skewers over an open flame and served on dark rye bread with red onions and baked beans.

ITALY

GUANCIALE Made from pork jowl or cheeks; *guancia* is Italian for "cheek." Guanciale is dry-cured with salt, pepper, and assorted spices. It takes three to five weeks to cure. It can be eaten on its own but is often used to flavor pasta dishes, sauces, soups, and stews.

LARDO Lardo is dense, white fatback that is cured with salt and various herbs. It's a delicacy of the northern Tuscany region of Colonnata, where it has been made since Roman times. Lardo di Colonnata is cured in marble tubs or basins that come from the neighboring region of Carrara. It is often served raw in thin slices that melt in your mouth like butter.

PANCETTA This Italian version of bacon, made from pork belly, is cured with salt and various spices, but it isn't smoked. It is rolled tightly and wrapped in a casing and then is dried for several weeks and as long as three months. Some versions are left flat. It is very flavorful, moister and less salty than American bacon.

PROSCIUTTO Made from the pig's hind leg or thigh, prosciutto takes anywhere from nine months to two years to make. It is dry-cured and unsmoked and is usually served uncooked in paper-thin slices.

SPECK ALTO ADIGE Italian speck is a delicacy from the Alto Adige region of northeast Italy. The cool, dry climate is ideal for curing meat and contributes to its much-loved flavor. Speck is similar to prosciutto. It's made from the hind leg and is dry-cured with salt and a variety of spices, such as juniper, garlic, pepper, bay leaves, nutmeg, and laurel. It is cold-smoked for only a few hours at a time, and then aged for several months. Like prosciutto, it is often served uncooked in paper-thin slices as charcuterie.

NETHERLANDS

ZEEUWS SPEK Dutch bacon that is traditionally seasoned with salt, pepper, and bay leaves. A traditional method of eating it is to serve it on whole-grain bread with mustard.

UNITED KINGDOM

BACK BACON, IRISH BACON, ENGLISH BACON
Back bacon is traditional British bacon that is sliced to include both the pork loin and the pork belly. It is usually unsmoked and is either wet- or dry-cured. Back bacon is like a cross between U.S. bacon and what is called "Canadian bacon" in the United States. It usually has a lean, oval part with a single strip of fat and therefore has a high meat-to-fat ratio. It is the most popular type of bacon in the United Kingdom and is the main ingredient in a "bacon sarnie" or a "bacon butty," a sandwich that includes strips of bacon doused in HP sauce or Worcestershire sauce. The Irish version may be saltier and smokier. A traditional Irish dish consists of Irish bacon with cabbage and a mustard or parsley sauce.

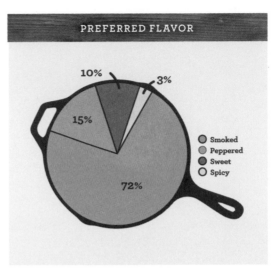

PREFERRED FLAVOR

10%
3%
15%
72%

- Smoked
- Peppered
- Sweet
- Spicy

In both England and Ireland, it is a main component of a "full English breakfast" or a "full Irish breakfast."

RASHER An individual slice of bacon or a serving of several strips of bacon.

STREAKY BACON The Brits, the Aussies, and the Kiwis refer to "American" bacon as streaky bacon. It gets its name from the "streaks" of fat and meat in the strips. In England, streaky bacon is usually leaner than it is in the United States.

UNITED STATES

TURKEY BACON, DUCK BACON, COCONUT BACON, AND SOY BACON Bacon that isn't from pork and should be avoided at all costs.

Metric Conversions

LINEAR MEASUREMENTS

$\frac{1}{16}$ inch	1.6 mm
$\frac{1}{8}$ inch	3 mm
1 inch	2.54 cm
1 foot	.3048 meters

MEASUREMENTS BY VOLUME

¼ cup	59 ml
⅓ cup	78 ml
½ cup	118 ml
⅔ cup	158 ml
¾ cup	177 ml
1 cup	237 ml
1½ cups	355 ml
1 teaspoon	5 ml
1 tablespoon	15 ml
1 quart	0.95 liter
1 gallon	3.79 liters

MEASUREMENTS BY WEIGHT

1 ounce	28.35 grams
1 pound	0.454 kg

TEMPERATURES

110°F	43°C
115°F	46°C
145°F	63°C
155°F	68°C
165°F	74°C
175°F	79°C
180°F	82°C
200°F	93°C
250°F	121°C
350°F	177°C
375°F	191°C
400°F	204°C
425°F	218°C
450°F	232°C

About the Authors

ROCCO LOOSBROCK

Rocco Loosbrock and his wife Yaneth started their business in 2001 with the simple idea that food should be fun and shared with family and friends. At an early age, Rocco was often in the kitchen with his Italian mother, Maria, baking bread and enjoying his family's very loud and opinionated conversations. In 1992, at the age of 19, Rocco joined the United States Army as a medic and served for four years, during which time he met his lovely wife and best friend. They have been married for 22 years and have two amazing children, Nalonie and Jimmy.

After leaving the military, Rocco worked at a local bank while attending classes and earned his Bachelor's degree in Management at Azusa Pacific University. During this time, he worked with small business owners and set a goal to one day own his own business, hoping it could involve his fill of wine. Soon Rocco was pairing swine with wine, and their business was born.

Rocco spends most of his time woodworking, cooking, and honing his green thumb for fresh ingredients for his kitchen. He enjoys cooking for his family and his friends. His wife just loves when he pretends he is on a TV show talking about food prep and adding anecdotal tidbits about his day.

SARA LEWIS

Sara Lewis received her BS in Graphic Design, but has always had a passion for baking and cooking. Sara has been happily bringing her creativity to the Bacon Freak team since 2011 and is often found drooling over bacon photography at her desk. It's a difficult job, but she knows that someone's gotta do it. When Sara isn't spending her time surrounded by bacon, she can be found whipping up delicious desserts, going to concerts, binge watching sci-fi shows or scary movies with her husband, and daydreaming about hosting dinner parties. She believes life can only be enjoyed surrounded by the people you love, eating the foods that make your soul happy.

DAWN HUBBARD

Dawn Hubbard is originally from Seattle and graduated with a Bachelor's degree in English Literature. Like many English Lit grads, she then worked in a totally unrelated field for 15 years. She was thrilled to land her job at Bacon Freak, which gave her the ability to finally utilize her creativity and writing skills. She currently lives in the greater Los Angeles area and is an avid foodie and beer connoisseur who appreciates LA's endless variety of restaurants, food trucks, and microbreweries. She is a huge anglophile and is a fan of Jane Austen and British TV. Combined with her love of reading, sewing, quilting, and cats, she is pretty much guaranteed to end up a crazy cat lady. She loves traveling with her husband and has visited a dozen different countries. Her ultimate life goal is to someday live in the UK or EU, where she will finally finish a book of short stories.

Acknowledgments

From Rocco "Boss Hog" Loosbrock

I have so many people that I want to thank who made this project possible. To start, I thank our literary agent, Marilyn Allen, who believed that we could create the best bacon cookbook ever written. Without her, this project never would have happened. A special thank you to the Sterling Publishing team, who shared my love for and obsession with bacon and believed in me and the Bacon Freak team. Thank you to my kids, Jimmy and Nalonie, and her friend Sam, who helped pack orders when we started in 2000 for the salary of a Slurpee at 7-Eleven. Special thanks to my parents, Jim and Maria, who helped us with shipping and receiving product and most importantly dropped off lunch and dinner at the office on those long days and nights. Huge thanks to my best friend and wife, Yaneth, who shared my vision, inspired me, and encouraged me each and every step of the way. Thank you so much. I love you!

A huge thanks to the whole Bacon Freak team, especially Michal Gurrola, who helped make our recipes even more bacony and brought the pages to life! Thank you all for making this dream a reality, and God bless.

From Sara Lewis

I thank my always-hungry husband, Jayme, along with my loving family for their encouragement and for always eating what I make even if it doesn't turn out quite right the first time.

From Dawn Hubbard

Thanks to my husband, Marc Hall, for your love and support.

Index

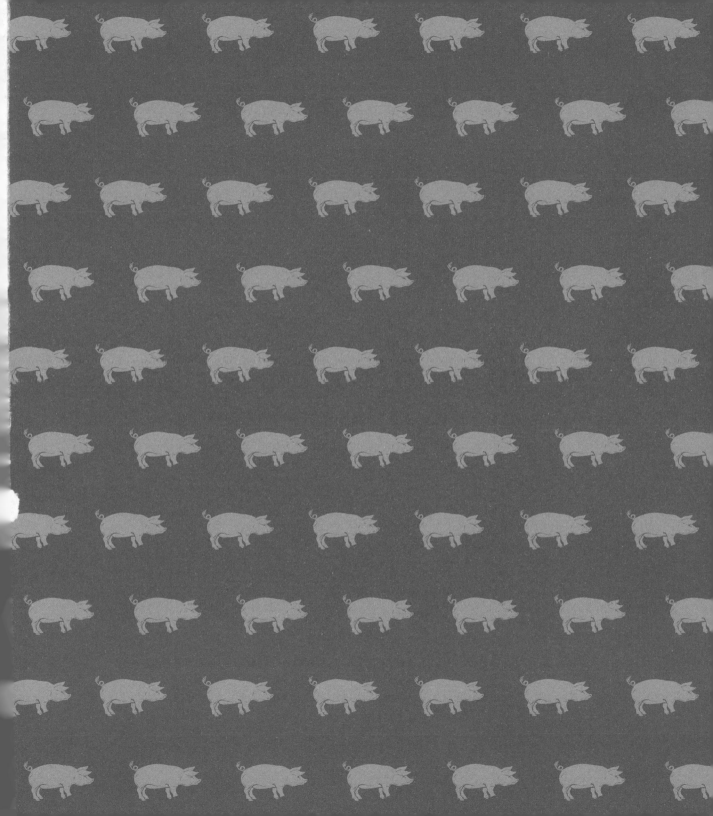

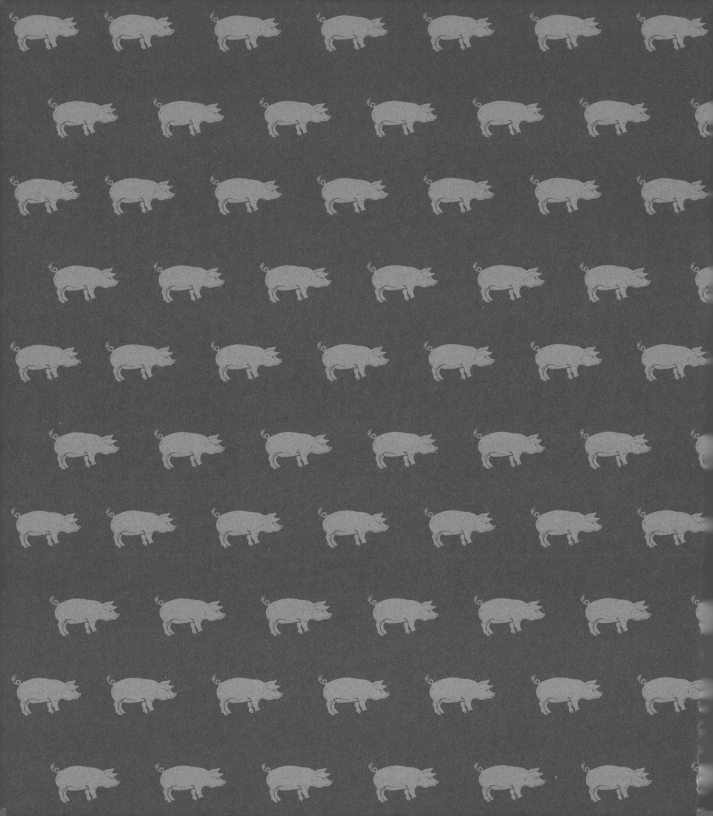